A USER'S GUIDE TO THE NESTLE-ALAND 28
GREEK NEW TESTAMENT

Society of Biblical Literature

Text-Critical Studies

Number 9

A USER'S GUIDE TO THE NESTLE-ALAND 28
GREEK NEW TESTAMENT

A USER'S GUIDE TO THE NESTLE-ALAND 28 GREEK NEW TESTAMENT

David Trobisch

Society of Biblical Literature
Atlanta

A USER'S GUIDE TO THE NESTLE-ALAND 28
GREEK NEW TESTAMENT

Printed on acid-free, recycled paper conforming to
ANSI/NISO Z39.48-1992 (R1997) and ISO 9706:1994
standards for paper permanence.

CONTENTS

PREFACE

In honor of two of its historical editors, the *Novum Testamentum Graece* is often simply referred to as the "Nestle-Aland." In the fall of 2012 it appeared in its 28th thoroughly revised edition. It was prepared for publication by the Institute for New Testament Textual Research in Münster, Westphalia, under the direction of Dr. Holger Strutwolf. This concise edition, which provides a survey of the manuscript evidence and a scholarly reconstruction of the oldest text of the Greek New Testament, has now grown to more than a thousand printed pages. In its new iteration, NA28 is easier to use than its predecessors, and it promises not only to continue playing a leading role for scholarly exegesis and academic instruction but also to supply the source text for Bible translators.

The present book is structured in three parts. The first part, "Structure and Intention of the Edition," has in mind readers who are using this edition of the Greek New Testament for the first time. Although knowledge of the Greek language is helpful, it is not a prerequisite to understand the narrative. The objective is to communicate the structure and concept of NA28 and also to create critical awareness for the problems and uncertainties encountered by reconstructions of the oldest Greek text. College students are the intended audience as well as a general readership interested in a better understanding of the references to text variations in Bible manuscripts that are found in most English translations of the New Testament and in exegetical publications. Exercises accompanying the explanations are designed to rehearse and apply important information. They may also prove helpful in the context of academic instruction. The solutions are given at the end of the book.

The second part, "Exercises and Learning Aids," demonstrates the application of the edition through specific examples. It explains technical terms and how to apply the information of the introduction, the technical apparatus, and the appendices. In an academic setting, such a level of knowledge and skill would be expected of a graduate student with a special interest in biblical literature.

The third part, "NA28 as an Edition for Scholars," provides an overview of the strengths and the limitations of NA28 for researchers and teachers who interpret the New Testament professionally. It also summarizes the important differences between the 28th edition and previous editions of the *Novum Testamentum Graece.*

Readers will need to have a copy of the 28th edition of the Nestle-Aland at hand to appreciate fully the detailed explanations. Unless otherwise indicated, numbers in parenthesis refer to pages of NA28.

My hope is that readers will find the book useful and that they will appreciate the effort of the colleagues who put together this concise critical edition of the Greek New Testament.

September 2013   David Trobisch

STRUCTURE AND INTENTION OF THE EDITION

1.1. The History of Transmission of the Greek New Testament

Between 5,500 and 6,000 handwritten copies with text from the New Testament are known today, and that number continues to increase. There is hardly a sentence of the New Testament that has the exact same wording in each of these exemplars. Why?

Most writings of the Greek Old Testament are based on old translations from Hebrew. When Jesus of Nazareth's last words on the cross are quoted in the Gospel according to Mark as "Eloi, Eloi, lema sabachthani?" the writer of the Gospel is quick to explain the meaning of this quote: "Which means, 'My God, my God, why have you forsaken me?'" (Mark 15:34). By making remarks like this, the Gospel writers inform their readers that Jesus did not speak Greek when he talked to peasants, fishermen, Pharisees, Sadducees, and scribes in Galilee or Judea. The writer makes readers aware that Jesus' speeches are presented in translation.

The simple observation that readers of the Christian Bible are aware of reading a translation explains in part why scribes and editors felt free to revise the Greek text during the fourteen centuries of its manuscript transmission. Greek was and is a living, spoken language, and many of these changes were designed to increase readability, to avoid possible misunderstandings, and to adapt expressions to the evolving vernacular. The same is practiced today, as our modern language editions are revised on a regular basis. Editors will typically replace awkward expressions with more familiar ones, update sentence structures to make them flow better for modern users, and correct an occasional error. Even venerated editions such as the King

James Version have seen numerous revisions to ensure the usability of this highly respected translation.

When it comes to the transmission of the Greek New Testament, scholars have identified several distinct Byzantine editions between the eighth and the fifteenth centuries. These so-called *recensions* permit scholars to group manuscripts together and to treat them as copies of the same archetype. For the earliest New Testament manuscripts (second to seventh centuries), however, such groups have not yet been determined with certainty.

Editorial changes are not the only explanation for the wealth of text variations. During the process of copying books, scribes may have made mistakes trying to decipher the old exemplar while producing a new one. It is indeed extremely difficult to copy text by hand without error.

The text of NA28 records the decisions of an international editorial committee that attempted to discern which of the existing variants document the oldest form of the New Testament and which of them originated later. NA28 therefore provides an *eclectic* text, as opposed to a *diplomatic* edition of a literary work. Diplomatic editions print the wording of a single manuscript and register variants from other manuscripts separately. The *Biblia Hebraica Stuttgartensia*, the scholarly edition of the Hebrew Bible, resembles in principle such a diplomatic edition. The editorial boards of the Nestle-Aland have changed over time. The strategy of textual decision-making had to be reconsidered as new manuscripts became accessible and methodological insights emerged. Since its first publication in 1898, Nestle-Aland has been produced in twenty-eight distinct editions.

Another goal of NA28 is to provide a wealth of pertinent information in a compact format. To achieve this, not all variants in all manuscripts are noted. Instead, the editors selected a number of passages in the text where they compared a selection of manuscripts. The result is presented in a concise, critical apparatus at the bottom of each page. For a comprehensive documentation of all variants in all manuscripts, scholars will have to access other resources, such as the *Editio Critica Maior* presently being prepared by the Institute of New Testament Textual Research (3* n. 1) as well. Hopefully, in the not-too-distant future, the documentation of variants will be made accessible in an electronic format as well.

𝔓⁴⁶: P.Mich.inv. 6238, 38; Verso. Romans 15:29–16:3. Image reproduced with the permission of the Papyrology Collection, Graduate Library, University of Michigan; Inventory number: P.Mich. inv. 6238.

1.2. The Manuscripts

Papyrus 46

The photograph of $\mathfrak{P}^{46}$ on page 3 is taken from the oldest surviving copy of the Letters of Paul. This manuscript is written on papyrus; NA28 references it as $\mathfrak{P}^{46}$ and dates it to the year "ca. 200" (794). The page shown presents text from Romans 15:29–16:3 and is now held at the University of Michigan in Ann Arbor.

When comparing the text of $\mathfrak{P}^{46}$ with the corresponding text printed in NA28 (Rom 15:19 is found on p. 514), differences are noticeable. $\mathfrak{P}^{46}$, like all older copies of the New Testament, is written in capital letters only, in so-called majuscules or uncials, whereas NA28 uses capital and small letters.

Furthermore, the text of $\mathfrak{P}^{46}$ displays almost no structural elements. The familiar chapter and verse numbers are missing, punctuation (e.g., commas, periods, question or exclamation marks) is not present, and the individual words are not separated by spaces.

Nomina Sacra in $\mathfrak{P}^{46}$

$\mathfrak{P}^{46}$, like all New Testament manuscripts, also contains a number of words that are written in a contracted form referred to as *nomina sacra* (literally translated, "sacred names"). This technical term refers to a set of words such as *God, Lord, Jesus,* and *Christ* that are written by noting only the first one or two and the last one or two letters of that word and eliminating the letters in the middle. The scribes marked these contractions by drawing a horizontal line across the top of the word.

Not all manuscripts note the same selection of words as *nomina sacra*, and it is not unusual for a scribe to contract a word in one place and to write out fully the same word in another place of the same manuscript.

The first two text lines of the page reproduced from $\mathfrak{P}^{46}$ contain three *nomina sacra*, all of which are written out fully in NA28.

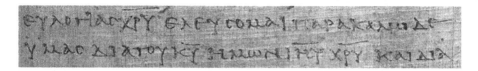

Transcription

ΕΥΛΟΓΙΑΣΧ̄Ρ̄Ῡ̄ΕΛΕΥΣΟΜΑΙΠΑΡΑΚΑΛΩΔΕ
ΥΜΑΣΔΙΑΤΟΥΚ̄Ῡ̄ΗΜΩΝῙΗ̄ῩΧ̄Ρ̄Ῡ̄ΚΑΙΔΙΑ

In transcription without *nomina sacra*, words are written out in full, spaces are inserted between the words, capital and small letters are used, and accents and breathing marks are indicated:

εὐλογίας Χριστοῦ ἐλεύσομαι παρακαλῶ δὲ
ὑμᾶς διὰ τοῦ κυρίου ἡμῶν Ἰησοῦ Χριστοῦ καὶ διὰ

Transcription without *nomina sacra* can be seen in this reproduction from NA28 (514):

ἐν ⌜πληρώματι εὐλογίας ᵀ Χριστοῦ ἐλεύσομαι.
30 Παρακαλῶ δὲ ὑμᾶς °[, ἀδελφοί,] διὰ τοῦ ᵀ κυρίου
ἡμῶν Ἰησοῦ Χριστοῦ καὶ διὰ τῆς ἀγάπης τοῦ πνεύματος

With the advent of the printing press in the fifteenth century, the standard editions of the Greek New Testament discontinued the practice of using *nomina sacra*. NA28 follows this convention.

The sample page also demonstrates that NA28 does not simply reproduce the text of the oldest surviving manuscript, namely, 𝔓⁴⁶. Comparison of the text of NA28 to that of 𝔓⁴⁶, for example, reveals that the editors not only structured the text by adding critical signs but also supplemented the Greek word αδελφοι, which is missing in 𝔓⁴⁶. The intention of this edition lies not in reproducing the "oldest text" presented in the oldest manuscript but in reconstructing the text of the hypothetical master copy from which all manuscripts derive, a text the editors refer to as the *initial text*.

Codex

The header of 𝔓⁴⁶ (see p. 3) displays two Greek numerals, ΛΗ, indicating a page number: 38. Almost all manuscripts of the New Testament are written in book form, *codices*, and not on scrolls. This is noteworthy because until the fourth century the ancient book trade predominantly used scrolls for literary texts. The codex was formed like a modern book by placing several sheets on top of each other, so-called *quires*. They were folded and bound together. The front and the back side of each page contained text. Scrolls, on the other hand, were written only on one side of the material. To produce a scroll, sheets were glued (papyrus) or sewn (parchment) together to form rolls of the desired length.

Papyrus, Majuscule, Minuscule

The Nestle-Aland distinguishes between manuscripts written on papyrus and manuscripts utilizing other materials. Most of the latter used parchment made from animal skins, but a few paper manuscripts from a later time exist as well. Manuscripts not written on papyrus are further categorized according to their handwriting: *majuscules* are written in capital letters only; *minuscules* are written using capital letters and small letters. Therefore, manuscripts are not only classified by the material they utilized; they are also distinguished by the type of script.

Papyri are noted in the apparatus with 𝔓 followed by a superscript numeral, as in 𝔓¹ 𝔓¹³ 𝔓⁴⁶. Majuscules are noted either by a Hebrew, Greek, or Latin capital letter or by a number beginning with a zero, such as ℵ B Ψ 0108. Minuscules are indicated by a simple number without the zero at the beginning followed by a period, such as 33. 81. 323.

Summary

Users of NA28 should be aware that the spaces between the words, the chapter and verse numbers, the paragraphs, the punctuation signs, and all other structural elements of the printed Greek text are not found in the oldest manuscripts but reflect editorial decisions. Translations and alternative editions of the Greek text may well vary from one another with respect to these structural markers. For example, the Nestle-Aland editions generally follow German comma rules, which may at times confuse English-speaking users.

Redactional elements of the manuscripts such as page numbers, line breaks, accents, and the notations of the *nomina sacra* are not reproduced in NA28. The orthography is standardized and reflects the scholarly practice of ancient Greek. Utilizing NA28 to reconstruct the exact spelling of a word in a specific manuscript is therefore impossible, unless this word is expressively noted in the apparatus.

Matthew 24:17–18

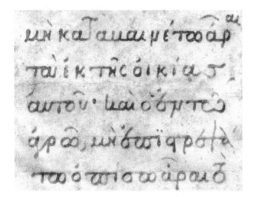

μη καταβαινετω αραι

τα εκ της οικιας

αυτου 18 και ο εν τω

αγρω μη επιστρεψα-

τω οπισω αραι το

Minuscule (lectionary) *l* 1372, fourteenth century. Digitally reproduced with the permission of the American Bible Society, New York.

Excursus: For Students without Knowledge of Greek

Greek was not the first language for most of the early readers of the New Testament and probably for many of the authors of New Testament writings. The New Testament was written in what is commonly described as *Koine Greek*, which means "common" Greek. This represented the *lingua franca* used for international communications throughout the Mediterranean world, comparable to the current use of English in Europe for business and academic communications. Much of the literature produced and commercially distributed in the Roman Empire during the first two centuries C.E. was written in Greek.

We cannot be sure how Greek was pronounced in antiquity. It has become common practice that the pronunciation of Greek text is done phonetically so that people from the same language group can transcribe it correctly when hearing it spoken. Accordingly, Germans will pronounce Greek words so that German listeners can easily distinguish each consonant and each vowel. Germans may, for instance, use *Umlaute* that are not available in the English language. On the other hand, Germans may not pronounce the Greek consonant theta (θ) as *th* (e.g., *this*) because the sound does not exist in the German language. Ancient Greek is pronounced differently by various modern language users, and none of their pronunciations claim to represent the ancient practice. Many scholars also agree that Modern Greek, as spoken in Greece today or as used internationally in the Greek Orthodox liturgy, should not be used as a pronunciation guideline for ancient Greek.

Greek Alphabet

Capital Letters	Small Letters	Letter Name	Transcription	Pronunciation as in:
A	α	*alpha*	a	f<u>a</u>ther
B	β	*beta*	b	
Γ	γ	*gamma*	g	<u>g</u>ift
Δ	δ	*delta*	d	
E	ε	*epsilon*	e	m<u>e</u>tropolitan
Z	ζ	*zeta*	z or dz	<u>z</u>ebra (at the beginning of a word), a<u>dz</u>e
H	η	*eta*	ē	ob<u>ey</u>
Θ	θ	*theta*	t	<u>t</u>heme
I	ι	*iota*	i	p<u>i</u>t (short) or magaz<u>i</u>ne (long, depending on accent)
K	κ	*kappa*	k	
Λ	λ	*lambda*	l	
M	μ	*mu*	m	

N	ν	*nu*	n	
Ξ	Ξ	*xi*	x	rela<u>x</u>
O	ο	*omicron*	o	<u>o</u>melet
Π	π	*pi*	p	
P	ρ	*rho*	r	
Σ	σ	*sigma*	s	
	ς	final *sigma*	s	used at end of word: Χριστος
T	τ	*tau*	t	
Υ	υ	*upsilon*	y; in diph-thongs u	t<u>u</u>be
Φ	φ	*phi*	ph	<u>ph</u>one
X	χ	*chi*	ch	<u>ch</u>emistry
Ψ	ψ	*psi*	ps	ho<u>ps</u>
Ω	ω	*omega*	ō	l<u>o</u>ne

Consonant Combinations

σχ	sch	<u>sch</u>ool
γγ	ng	a<u>ng</u>el
γκ	nk	u<u>nc</u>le
γξ	nx	tha<u>nks</u>
γχ	nch	a<u>nch</u>ovies

Diphthongs

αι	ai	<u>ai</u>sle
ᾳ	a	like regular *alpha*
αυ	au	cr<u>ow</u>d
ει	ei	h<u>ei</u>ght
ευ	eu	f<u>eu</u>d

η	ē	like regular *eta*
ηυ	ēu	f<u>eu</u>d
οι	oi	v<u>oi</u>d
ου	ou	gr<u>ou</u>p
υι	ui	s<u>ui</u>te
ῳ	ō	l<u>o</u>ne

Accents

´	acute	
`	grave	The syllable with the accent is stressed.
˜	circumflex	

Breathing Marks

If a word begins with a vowel, a breathing mark (*spiritus*) is written over that vowel.

᾿	*spiritus lenis*	not pronounced
῾	*spiritus asper*	pronounced as the *h* in *hypocrite*
ῥ	*circumflex*	*Rho* (P, ρ) receives a *spiritus asper* (ῥ) at the beginning of a word; it is transcribed as *rh* but pronounced the same as regular *rho*, as in *rheumatism*.

Reading Exercise

a. Go to page 12 and copy the first four lines of the Greek text by hand (1 Cor 16:21–24), ignoring accents and breathing marks (→ solution).[1]

---

1. Exercises and questions marked (→ solution) have answers provided at the end of this book.

b. Check every word that begins with a vowel. If the vowel carries a *spiritus asper*, add the breathing mark so you do not forget to pronounce an aspirated *h* at the beginning of the word (→ solution).

c. Underline the vowel or diphthong of each word that carries the accent indicating the emphasis or stress when you read it out loud (→ solution).

d. Using the tables above, pronounce each word and read the text out loud. Confirm the following:

— Do you distinguish the *eta* from the *epsilon* and the *omicron* (short) from the *omega* (long) clearly enough for listeners to hear a difference?

— Do you recognize ου as a diphthong and pronounce it correctly?

— Do you pronounce the *spiritus asper* as *h*?

— Do you put the stress on the syllable that carries the accent?

Writing Exercise

a. Referring to the tables above as needed, transcribe the following names in Greek letters; check your work against the names given in NA28: Abraham (Matt 1:1); Isaac and Jacob (Matt 1:2); Judas, Tamar, and Aram (Matt 1:3); Ruth (Matt 1:5); Joseph and Jesus (Matt 1:16).

b. Copy the sample text of 1 Cor 16:21–24 once more by hand. This time, write the text in capital letters, ignoring accents and breathing marks (→ solution).

1.3. LOOKING AT ONE PAGE OF NA28

The printed page containing text from the end of 1 Corinthians and the beginning of 2 Corinthians looks like this:

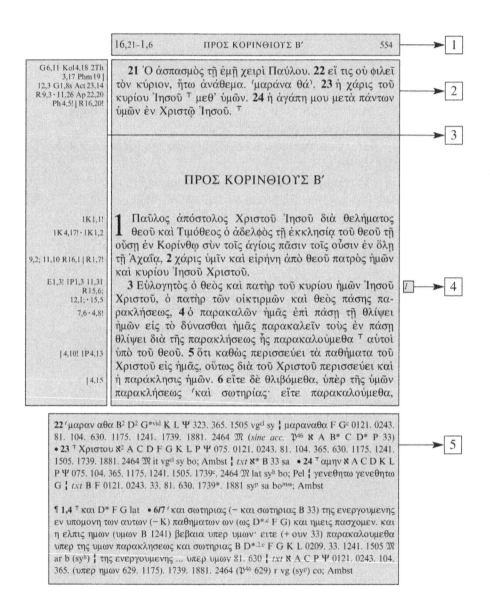

| 16,21–1,6 | ΠΡΟΣ ΚΟΡΙΝΘΙΟΥΣ Β′ | 554 |

G6,11 Kol4,18 2Th
3,17 Phm 19 |
12,3 G1,8s Act 23,14
R9,3 · 11,26 Ap 22,20
Ph 4,5! | R 16,20!

21 Ὁ ἀσπασμὸς τῇ ἐμῇ χειρὶ Παύλου. **22** εἴ τις οὐ φιλεῖ τὸν κύριον, ἤτω ἀνάθεμα. ʿμαράνα θά᾽. **23** ἡ χάρις τοῦ κυρίου Ἰησοῦ ᵀ μεθ᾽ ὑμῶν. **24** ἡ ἀγάπη μου μετὰ πάντων ὑμῶν ἐν Χριστῷ Ἰησοῦ. ᵀ

ΠΡΟΣ ΚΟΡΙΝΘΙΟΥΣ Β′

1K1,1!
1K4,17! · 1K1,2

9,2; 11,10 R16,1 | R1,7!

E1,3! 1P1,3 11,31
R15,6;
12,1; · 15,5
7,6 · 4,8!

| 4,10! 1P4,13

| 4,15

1 Παῦλος ἀπόστολος Χριστοῦ Ἰησοῦ διὰ θελήματος θεοῦ καὶ Τιμόθεος ὁ ἀδελφὸς τῇ ἐκκλησίᾳ τοῦ θεοῦ τῇ οὔσῃ ἐν Κορίνθῳ σὺν τοῖς ἁγίοις πᾶσιν τοῖς οὖσιν ἐν ὅλῃ τῇ Ἀχαΐᾳ, **2** χάρις ὑμῖν καὶ εἰρήνη ἀπὸ θεοῦ πατρὸς ἡμῶν καὶ κυρίου Ἰησοῦ Χριστοῦ.

3 Εὐλογητὸς ὁ θεὸς καὶ πατὴρ τοῦ κυρίου ἡμῶν Ἰησοῦ Χριστοῦ, ὁ πατὴρ τῶν οἰκτιρμῶν καὶ θεὸς πάσης παρακλήσεως, **4** ὁ παρακαλῶν ἡμᾶς ἐπὶ πάσῃ τῇ θλίψει ἡμῶν εἰς τὸ δύνασθαι ἡμᾶς παρακαλεῖν τοὺς ἐν πάσῃ θλίψει διὰ τῆς παρακλήσεως ἧς παρακαλούμεθα ᵀ αὐτοὶ ὑπὸ τοῦ θεοῦ. **5** ὅτι καθὼς περισσεύει τὰ παθήματα τοῦ Χριστοῦ εἰς ἡμᾶς, οὕτως διὰ τοῦ Χριστοῦ περισσεύει καὶ ἡ παράκλησις ἡμῶν. **6** εἴτε δὲ θλιβόμεθα, ὑπὲρ τῆς ὑμῶν παρακλήσεως ʿκαὶ σωτηρίας· εἴτε παρακαλούμεθα,

22 ʿμαραν αθα B² D² G*ᵛⁱᵈ K L Ψ 323. 365. 1505 vgᶜˡ sy | μαραναθα F Gᶜ 0121. 0243. 81. 104. 630. 1175. 1241. 1739. 1881. 2464 𝔐 (*sine acc.* 𝔓⁴⁶ ℵ A B* C D* P 33) • **23** ᵀ Χριστου ℵ² A C D F G K L P Ψ 075. 0121. 0243. 81. 104. 365. 1175. 1241. 1505. 1739. 1881. 2464 𝔐 it vgᶜˡ sy bo; Ambst ¦ *txt* ℵ* B 33 sa • **24** ᵀ αμην ℵ A C D K L P Ψ 075. 104. 365. 1175. 1241. 1505. 1739ᶜ. 2464 𝔐 lat syʰ bo; Pel ¦ γενεθητω γενεθητω G ¦ *txt* B F 0121. 0243. 33. 81. 630. 1739*. 1881 syᵖ sa boᵐˢˢ; Ambst

¶ **1,4** ᵀ και D* F G lat • **6/7** ʿκαι σωτηριας (– και σωτηριας B 33) της ενεργουμενης εν υπομονη των αυτων (– K) παθηματων ων (ως D*·ᶜ F G) και ημεις πασχομεν. και η ελπις ημων (υμων B 1241) βεβαια υπερ υμων· ειτε (+ ουν 33) παρακαλουμεθα υπερ της υμων παρακλησεως και σωτηριας B D*·²ᶜ F G K L 0209. 33. 1241. 1505 𝔐 ar b (syʰ) ¦ της ενεργουμενης … υπερ υμων 81. 630 ¦ *txt* ℵ A C P Ψ 0121. 0243. 104. 365. (υπερ ημων 629. 1175). 1739. 1881. 2464 (𝔓⁴⁶ 629) r vg (syᵖ) co; Ambst

[1] The top margin displays the page number of the edition, the Greek title of the respective writing, and the chapter and verse numbers as a running header.

[2] The Greek text is printed with justified margins in the middle of the page.

[3] The outer margin registers text parallels.

[4] The inner margin indicates alternatives of structuring the text as found in parts of the manuscript tradition.

[5] The bottom of the page presents the apparatus that documents variants in the manuscripts.

In order to use the apparatus of NA28 successfully, readers must familiarize themselves with the Greek alphabet and understand the most common critical signs used in the apparatus. They also need to know where to find explanations for all abbreviations and where to get basic information about the text witnesses.

Exercise

a. Identify the page containing Mark 10:46 by thumbing through NA28 from the beginning until the running header changes to "KATA MAPKON." Then look at the chapter and verse numbers noted in the outer margin of the header until you reach the page containing Mark 10:46, where the story of the healing of Bartimaeus's blindness begins.

b. Look for the notation of parallels in the outer margin. Where is this story found in Matthew and Luke (→ solution)?

c. Identify the beginning of verse 46 in the Greek text. The number **46** is printed in bold.

d. Immediately following the verse number is a critical sign that looks like a square (□). It marks the beginning of the phrase Καὶ ἔρχονται εἰς Ἰεριχώ ("And they came to Jericho"). After these four words, a small superscript backslash (ˋ) marks the end of the reference. These signs indicate that the four Greek words are missing in some of the text witnesses. Go down to the apparatus below and identify the beginning of the critical notes for verse 46. The little square (▫) is repeated there. In which of the text witnesses are the four Greek words missing (→ solution)?

1.4. STRUCTURE OF THE EDITION

NA28 is structured in three parts: introduction, critical text with apparatus, and the appendices. Information about how the critical text and the apparatus were established is given at the beginning of the book; information about textual witnesses is provided at the end of the book (appendices).

1.4.1. Introduction and Main Body with Text and Apparatus

Critical Signs

If two versions of a text are compared to each other, their differences can be organized in four categories: additions, deletions, replacements, and rearrangements. Users of NA28 should therefore familiarize themselves with the signs indicating these major differences in this edition.

Omissions

°   The following word was omitted. The critical sign looks like an *o* for "omitted."

▫ ... `   Several words were omitted. The beginning and the end of the omission is marked.

Insertions

τ   Text was inserted at this point.

Replacements

Replacing words with other words technically involves a deletion as well as an addition; sometimes such variants are noted in that manner. Most of the time, however, space is saved by noting this kind of variant as a replacement.

⌐   The following word was replaced.

⌐ ... ⌐   Several words were replaced.

Rearrangements

^{s} ... ^{2} The words between these signs are rearranged.

Exercise

a. The example below indicates that the text of the New Revised Standard Version was put in the text line and that the apparatus notes text variants in the New International Version of the same passage. Reconstruct the wording of the NIV (→ solution).

Text (NRSV Jude 1–2): Jude, a servant of Jesus Christ and $^{\top}$brother of James, To those who $^{\ulcorner}$are called, who are $^{\ulcorner1}$beloved in God the Father and kept $^{\circ}$safe for Jesus Christ: $^{\circ1}$May mercy, peace, and love be yours in abundance.
Apparatus: $^{\top}$ a NIV | $^{\ulcorner}$have been NIV | $^{\ulcorner1}$loved NIV | $^{\circ}$NIV | $^{\circ1}$NIV.

b. Now create an apparatus for Jude 3 (included below) by placing the NIV in the text and noting the text differences of the NRSV in the apparatus. Pay attention to the following conventions: (a) If the same sign is used more than once, add a number after the sign. For example, mark the first omission with $^{\circ}$, the second omission of a word with $^{\circ1}$, and the next one with $^{\circ2}$, and so on. (b) Separate the entries in the apparatus with a line: |. Ignore variations in punctuation for this exercise.

NIV: Dear friends, although I was very eager to write to you about the salvation we share, I felt compelled to write and urge you to contend for the faith that was once for all entrusted to God's holy people.
NRSV: Beloved, while eagerly preparing to write to you about the salvation we share, I find it necessary to write and appeal to you to contend for the faith that was once for all entrusted to the saints. (→ solution)

Organization of Entries in the Apparatus

The entries reference the traditional verse numbers.

- •   The beginning of the verse is marked with a bold dot followed by a number also printed in bold (see the entry for 1 Cor 16:23 in the sample page above: • **23**).
- ...|...   If a verse has more than one noted variant, for example, an omission at one place and an addition at another, then the entries are separated by a vertical line.
- ...¦...   However, if there is more than one variant noted at the same place in the text, for example, an addition in one manuscript but an omission at the same location in another manuscript, then these readings are separated by a broken vertical line (see 1 Cor 16:22, 23, 24).
- ¦ txt   This critical sign at the end of an entry introduces a list of witnesses that support the wording as it is printed in the text line of the edition.

Arrangement of Witnesses in the Apparatus

Witnesses to a variant are always listed in the same order.

(1) The Greek manuscripts are mentioned first. They are organized in three categories: papyri, majuscules, and minuscules.

- a.   The papyri are noted with a "𝔓" followed by a superscript numeral, $\mathfrak{P}^1$ $\mathfrak{P}^{13}$ $\mathfrak{P}^{46}$.
- b.   The majuscules are listed next. Each one is denoted either by a capital letter from the Hebrew, Latin, or Greek alphabet or by a zero followed by a number: א B Ψ 0108.
- c.   Minuscules are referenced by numbers (without a preceding zero) followed by a period: 33. 81. 323.

(2) After the Greek manuscripts, the early translations of the New Testament (e.g., Latin, Syriac, and Coptic) are noted. See page 35 for more information about these translations.

(3) The entry comes to a close by a list of quotes from this passage found in early Christian literature. This list is separated from the previous notations by a semicolon ";" (see pp. 35–36 below).

Exercise

c. The entry for Acts 1:10 presents the following list of witnesses: "𝔓⁵⁶ᶜ ℵ A B C* Ψ 81. 323. 945. 1175 lat; Eus." Identify which of these witnesses are minuscules, majuscules, papyri, versions, and citations (→ solution).

1.4.2. Appendices

Greek Manuscripts (Appendix I, A: Codices Graeci)

The first part of this appendix provides information about the manuscripts used to construct the text and the apparatus of NA28 (concerning the second part of Appendix I, see p. 38). This information is presented in four columns.

*𝔓126	IV	Firenze, Ist. Pap. «G. Vitelli», PSI inv. 2176	H 13,12-13.19-20
*𝔓127	V	Oxford, Ashmolean Mus.; P.Oxy. 4968	Act 10,32-35.40-45; 11,2-5; 11,30-12,3.5.7-9; 15,29-30.34-41; 16,1-4.13-40; 17,1-10
*ℵ 01	IV	London, Brit. Libr., Add. 43725	eapr
*A 02	V	London, Brit. Libr., Royal 1 D. VIII	eapr (vac. Mt 1,1-25,6; J 6,50-8,52; 2K 4,14-12,6)
*B 03	IV	Città del Vaticano, Bibl. Vat., Vat. gr. 1209	eap (vac. 1T-Phm; H 9,14-fin.)
*C 04	V	Paris, Bibl. Nat., Gr. 9	eapr (vac. Mt 1,1-2; 5,15-7,5; 17,26-18,28; 22,21-23,17; 24,10-45; 25,30-26,22; 27,11-46; 28,15-fin.; Mc 1,1-17; 6,32-8,5; 12,30-13,19; L 1,1-2; 2,5-42; 3,21-4,25; 6,4-36; 7,17-8,28; 12,4-19,42; 20,28-21,20; 22,19-23,25; 24,7-45; J 1,1-3; 1,41-3,33; 5,17-6,38; 7,3-8,34; 9,11-11,7; 11,47-13,7; 14,8-16,21; 18,36-20,25; Act 1,1-2; 4,3-5,34; 6,8; 10,43-13,1; 16,37-20,10; 21,31-22,20; 23,18-24,15; 26,19-27,16; 28,5-fin.; R 1,1-2; 2,5-3,21; 9,6-10,15; 11,31-13,10; 1K 1,1-2; 7,18-9,6; 13,8-15,40; 2K 1,1-2; 10,8-fin.; G 1,1-20; E 1,1-2,18; 4,17-fin.; Ph 1,1-22; 3,5-fin.; Kol 1,1-2; 1Th 1,1; 2,9-fin.; 2Th; 1T 1,1-3,9; 5,20-fin.; 2T 1,1-2; Tt 1,1-2; Phm 1-2; H 1,1-2,4; 7,26-9,15; 10,24-12,15; Jc 1,1-2; 4,2-fin.; 1P 1,1-2; 4,5-fin.; 2P 1,1; 1J 1,1-2; 4,3-fin.; 2J; 3J 1-2; Jd 1,1-2; 3,20-5,14; 7,14-17; 8,5-9,16; 10,10-11,3; 16,13-18,2; 19,5-fin.)
*D 05	V	Cambridge, Univ. Libr., Nn. 2. 41	ea (vac. Mt 1,1-20; 6,20-9,2; 27,2-12; J 1,16-3,26; Act 8,29-10,14; 21,2-10.16-18; 22,10-20.29-fin.; Jc-Jd [Mt 3,7-16; Mc 16,15-20; J 18,14-20,13 suppl.])
*D 06	VI	Paris, Bibl. Nat., Gr. 107 AB	p (vac. R 1,1-6; [1,27-30; 1K 14,13-22 suppl.])
E 07	VIII	Basel, Univ. Bibl., AN III 12	e†
*E 08	VI	Oxford, Bodl. Libr., Laud. Gr. 35	a (vac. Act 26,29-28,26; Jc-Jd)
*F 010	IX	Cambridge, Trin. Coll., B. XVII. 1	p (vac. R 1,2-3,18; 1K 3,8-15; 6,7-14; Kol 2,1-8; Phm 21-fin.; H)

Appendix I. A: Codices Graeci (799).

Column 1

The first column (ms. nr.) indicates the abbreviated designation of the manuscript as it is listed in the apparatus. The witnesses are arranged in the sequence papyri, majuscules, and minuscules.

Why are some majuscules noted in the apparatus only with a capital letter and others only with a number? The letter designations were established at a time when so few majuscules were known that the letters of the alphabet seemed sufficient to reference a specific manuscript. Today, however, with more than three hundred registered majuscules, every manuscript has been assigned a number that begins with a zero. This number is printed next to the traditional letter in the first column.

An asterisk (*) indicates that the editors considered this manuscript so significant that its reading is consistently cited in the apparatus.

Columns 2 and 3

The second column (saec. = *saeculum*, "century") gives an approximate date of the manuscript by indicating the century with a Roman numeral. These dates serve only for an initial orientation, since such assessments are occasionally heavily contested among scholars.

The third column (bibliotheca) lists the city and institution where the manuscript was kept when NA28 went to print. It also notes the calling number of the specific library.

For example, the entry for 058, "Wien, Österr. Nat. Bibl., Pap. G. 39782," indicates that this manuscript is held in Vienna ("Wien") at the Austrian National Library ("Österr. Nat. Bibl.") under the call number Pap. G. 39782.

Column 4

The fourth column (cont. = *continent*, "they contain") describes the contents of the manuscript, often using only four letters: e, a, p, and r. These four letters refer to the four collection units of New Testament manuscripts.

Most printed editions of the Greek New Testament begin with the four Gospels, followed by Acts, the Letters of Paul, the Catholic Letters, and end with the Revelation of John. It seems that the New Testament was perceived in antiquity as one literary work consisting of four volumes. Most manuscripts contain only one of these volumes, and some have two or three combined, but only very few manuscripts (less than 1 percent) preserve all twenty-seven writings. This is the reason why the editors of NA28 chose to describe the original contents of a manuscript by using four letters.

e   Four Gospels (*evangelium*).

p   Letters of Paul. This collection consists of fourteen letters. As far as the manuscript transmission is concerned, the Letter to the Hebrews is part of the Pauline corpus.

a   Acts and the Catholic Letters. It may come as a surprise to realize that Acts and the Catholic Letters are referenced with only a single letter. Modern printed editions usually present the Letters of Paul between Acts and the Catholic Letters. However, the four oldest witnesses that originally contained all the writings of the New Testament (ℵ, A, B, C; see p. 20 below) present Acts before the Catholic Letters. Later manuscripts often display our modern sequence. It seems that editors of the Byzantine editions rearranged the writings and inserted the Letters of Paul between Acts and the Catholic Letters, although their motivation is not entirely clear. The earliest prints of the sixteenth century produced the Greek text from late Byzantine manuscripts, and from these printed editions it was adopted into the first Nestle edition in 1898. Although NA28 reconstructs a pre-Byzantine text, it does not arrange the writings of the New Testament in the pre-Byzantine sequence.

r   Revelation of John.

For example, the entry for manuscript 221 "ap" indicates that this minuscule contains Acts, the Catholic Letters, and the Letters of Paul. However, it is not possible to say whether the Letters of Paul in 221 stand at the beginning or at the end of this manuscript or whether the collection was inserted between Acts and the Catholic Letters. We also cannot tell from this entry whether Hebrews is presented between 2 Thessalonians and 1 Timothy or whether it follows after Philemon.

Since many manuscripts have suffered losses, the editors often note which passages are missing. A missing text is indicated with "vac." (*vacat*, "it is missing"). The entry for majuscule Δ 037 "e (vac. J 19,17–35)" indicates that this manuscript contains the Four Gospels with the exception of John 19:17–35.

When manuscripts consist of only a few fragments, the editors do not use the abbreviations e a p r; they only list those passages contained in the manuscript.

The Four Oldest Manuscripts of the Entire New Testament

Four manuscripts considered especially helpful for the reconstruction of the initial text of the Greek New Testament are consistently cited in NA28. All four are majuscules dated to the fourth and fifth centuries. All of them originally contained the Old Testament as well, which makes them the oldest existing copies not only of the New Testament but also of the Greek Christian Bible.

- ℵ 01 (fourth century). This manuscript is called *Codex Sinaiticus,* named after St. Catherine's Monastery of Mount Sinai, where it was discovered by Konstantin von Tischendorf in 1844. Today it is held at the British Library in London.
- A 02 (fifth century). *Codex Alexandrinus* is also part of the collection in the British Library in London. In 1627 Kyrillos Loukaris, Patriarch of Alexandria, gave it as a present to King Charles I.
- B 03 (fourth century). Since this manuscript is held at the Vatican Apostolic Library, it is referred to in exegetical literature simply as *Codex Vaticanus.*
- C 04 (fifth century). Today this manuscript is held at the National Library of France in Paris and contains tractates of the Syrian church father Ephrem. It is called *Codex Ephraemi rescriptus* because the pages used for this codex were taken from a fifth-century Christian Bible, the ink was washed off, and the book was rewritten (*rescriptus*) and rebound.

Exercises

a.   The Appendix I sample above (p. 17) describes the content of manuscript B (03) as "eap (vac. 1T–Phm; H 9,14–fin.)." Which writings are missing in manuscript B (→ solution)?

b.   Appendix I. A: Codices Graeci lists the following: two different manuscripts with the letter D (05, 06), two manuscripts with E (07, 08), three manuscripts with H (013, 014, 015), two with K (017, 018), two with L (019, 020), and two with P (024, 025). Each of these cases uses the same letters for manuscripts that are not related to each other. The manuscript D, for which variants are listed in Acts 1:1, is a different manuscript than manuscript D for which variants are listed in Rom 1:8. Nevertheless, the reference is precise. Why are the editors able to use the same letter to designate different manuscripts (→ solution)?

c.   Look up the entry for manuscript 036. Decipher the information of all four columns and write it out in complete sentences (→ solution).

List of Abbreviations

Among the material provided in the appendices, the list of abbreviations is especially useful (Appendix IV: Signa et Abbreviationes, 879–90). It is more comprehensive than in previous editions of the Nestle-Aland. For the first time, German as well as English translations are provided for Latin terms, each followed by a brief explanation (see 885–90). Longer explanations of signs and abbreviations, however, are provided in the introduction to NA28.

Exercises

a.   Identify the entry "sy^{hmg}" in the list of abbreviations. On which page of the introduction is this abbreviation explained (→ solution)?

b. Identify the entry "v.l." in the list of abbreviations. On which page of the introduction is this abbreviation explained (→ solution)?

Maps

The insides of the front and back covers provide color maps. The maps inside the front cover show Palestine at the time of the Old and the New Testaments. The two maps inside the back cover depict the Middle East at the time of the Old Testament and the Mediterranean region during the first century, indicating the journeys of the apostle Paul as narrated in Acts.

1.5. EVALUATING VARIANTS

The reconstructed initial text is reproduced in the text line, and the variants are registered in the apparatus. However, to keep the format of this concise edition compact, the editors do not discuss why specific readings are placed in the apparatus while others are placed in the text line.

The following explains two general rules that inform text-critical decisions. They are briefly explained here in order to provide a first orientation for readers who have never before been confronted with critical editions of texts from antiquity. However, the method used to construct the text of NA28 is much more refined. The so-called Coherence-Based Genealogical Method (CBGM) was developed over a period of many years, and it provides the methodological foundation for the *Editio Critica Maior* (see pp. 53–54).

The shorter reading is the better reading (*lectio brevior*).

Manuscripts of literary texts display a tendency to combine competing readings. When editors and scribes became aware of text variations, they usually preferred preserving all readings to favoring one reading over another. Two variants are often simply combined.

For example, the end of Luke describes the disciples returning to Jerusalem. One text tradition says, "they were continually in the temple blessing God" (Luke 24:53). The Greek word for "blessing" is ευλογουντες. Some manuscripts have αινουντες, which is synonymous with ευλογουντες. Later traditions simply add και ("and") between the variants, leaving translators with the challenge of searching for two synonyms. The King James Version of 1611 was based on manuscripts with this conflate reading, so it translated the sentence: "they were continually in the temple, praising *and* blessing God."

Using this strategy, however, was not always possible. The list of the twelve disciples (Matt 10:3) depicts Thaddaeus (θαδδαιος) as the tenth disciple in some manuscripts; other manuscripts, however, name him Lebbaeus (Λεββαιος). Listing both names would bring the count of Jesus' disciples to the unacceptable number of thirteen. The apparatus of NA28 records several creative solutions to this dilemma: "Lebbaeus who is also called Thaddaeus" (Λ. ο επικληθεις Θ.), "Thaddaeus who is also called Lebbaeus" (Θ. ο επικληθεις Λ.), or just "Lebbaeus who is also Thaddaeus" (Λ. ο και Θ). The translators of the King James Version go with "Lebbaeus, whose surname was Thaddaeus," which, strictly speaking, is not recorded in any of the variants.

The observation that two variants are often combined to a conflate reading recognizes the fact that only one of those two readings represents the initial text. The Latin expression for this rule, *lectio brevior potior,* indicates that the shorter reading is the preferred reading.

Conflate readings do not occur only in Bible manuscripts but are typical for the manuscript transmission of any literary text from antiquity. In some ways the practice expresses the interest to preserve known variants for future generations of readers. This goal is shared with the editors of NA28. However, the Nestle-Aland edition notes the variants in the apparatus and does not include them in the text.

Although the *lectio brevior* rule insists that one of the combined readings must be older, it does not determine which one it is. For making that decision, the second general rule may prove helpful.

The more difficult reading is the better reading (*lectio difficilior*).

When Bible translations are revised, one of the goals is to adapt the language to contemporary usage. Expressions, phrases, and sentence structures that modern readers deem old-fashioned and outdated are replaced with familiar ones. For example, the first sentence of the New Testament in the first edition of the 1611 KJV reads, "THE booke of the generation of Jesus Christ, the sonne of David, the sonne of Abraham." However, a copy in bookstores today will read, "The book of the generation of Jesus Christ, the son of David, the son of Abraham." Both copies are called the King James Version by their publishers. Sometimes, positive connotations of certain words may have shifted, and the identical word now has attained a negative bias.

Greek was a living language during the fourteen hundred years in which the text of the New Testament was transmitted by hand, and Greek is still spoken today. It is more likely that editors would make a text easier to understand than making it intentionally more difficult. This observation is applicable to the manuscript tradition of any ancient Greek text and has informed the second general rule: if one competing variant is more difficult to understand than the other, the more difficult reading is to be preferred. The Latin expression of this rule is *lectio difficilior potior*.

Common Misconceptions

Sometimes *lectio brevior* is thought of as simply determining the lengths of the competing variants and then preferring the reading with the least amount of characters. This would be a profound misconception. The rule only applies to two readings that are superficially combined. Ideally, both readings are reflected in the manuscript tradition, but in many cases only the conflation and one of the two readings has survived; in other cases only the conflation is documented, and exegetes would have to infer two older variants from the surviving evidence.

When it comes to editorial additions, which are common in the manuscript tradition (e.g., after Mark 16:8 or Rom 14:23), the argument for the shorter text is often strengthened through the *lectio difficilior* principle.

Another misconception is that a manuscript dating from an earlier time warrants a better text. Indeed, the opposite is often true. Some of the oldest papyri survived only because they were discarded. Furthermore, a first copy may have the same probability of conveying scribal errors as a copy dating from a later time.

It remains insignificant whether a manuscript was written in majuscules or minuscules or whether it was written on papyrus or parchment. NA28 itself is a good example to illustrate this point: it is printed on paper, it uses capital and small letters, and it belongs to the most recent versions of the New Testament. Nevertheless, the editors will insist that their edition preserves the oldest recoverable text of the New Testament and that it is better than any single manuscript or any older print edition, including the 27th edition of the Nestle-Aland.

1.6. CONCLUDING QUESTIONS

Before engaging the next section of the book, make sure you can answer the following questions.

a. How are the text witnesses arranged in the apparatus (→ solution)?
b. Where does NA28 explain the abbreviations used in the critical apparatus (→ solution)?
c. Where in NA28 does one find information about Greek manuscripts (→ solution)?
d. What are the four oldest manuscripts that originally contained the entire Old and New Testament? What is the scholarly consensus for their dates? Where are they kept today (→ solution)?

EXERCISES AND LEARNING AIDS

The second part of this guide is for users who are able to translate Greek texts from the New Testament with the help of standard resources. The objective of this section is to deepen these readers' basic understanding of NA28 and to help develop practical skills for scholarly use.

The first and most important step for users is to familiarize themselves with the introduction by the editors.

2.1. Questions about the Introduction of NA28

The foreword (vii–viii) and introduction to the edition (46*–88*) contain a wealth of information. I recommend that one first work through each section indicated by the subheadings before trying to answer the related questions. The number in parentheses refers to the relevant page. In addition, the correct answers for all these questions can be found at the end of this book.

Preface (vii–viii)

    a. For most New Testament writings the editors of NA28 adopted the text of the 27th edition without changes, but for one section of the New Testament they introduced text changes. Which writings are affected? (vii).

    b. Has the marginal apparatus of references been revised for the entire edition or only for part of NA28? (vi)

About the History of the Edition (46*–53*)

    a. What two tasks did the editors try to accomplish when revising the apparatus? (48*)

   b. Why did the editors make several changes to the text of the Catholic Letters? (48*)

   c. How often was the text of the Catholic Letters changed from the text of the 27th edition? (50*–51*)

   d. Within the Catholic Letters, the rhomb (◆) is applied as a critical symbol. What does this symbol indicate? (51*)

   e. The sign 𝔐 refers to the "Majority Text" in the apparatus but is not used in the apparatus to the Catholic Letters. Instead, a new abbreviation is introduced that describes the editorial history of the New Testament more precisely. Which abbreviation?

The Text of the Edition (54*–55*)

   a. The editors of NA28 provide an eclectic text in their critical edition. How is such a text constructed? (54*)

   b. What are "external" and "internal" criteria to discern which of several variants is the oldest? (54*)

   c. What is the name of the method that the editors applied for the Catholic Letters? (54*)

   d. What do the square brackets […] indicate, and why are they not used for the Catholic Letters? (54*)

   e. What do the double-brackets ⟦…⟧ indicate? (55*)

   f. How are quotations from the Old Testament printed? (55*)

The Critical Apparatus (55*–81*)

   a. What is the difference between a "positive" apparatus and a "negative" apparatus? (55*–56*)

   b. What does a raised colon (˙) indicate? (57*)

   c. When is the sign ˢ…ᶻ used? (57*)

   d. What is the function of the sign •? (57*)

   e. Where are the variants of Greek witnesses quoted that are listed in parentheses (…)? (58*)

   f. What kind of variant is noted in brackets […]? (58*)

g. The old translations of the New Testament (i.e., the versions) are always listed in the apparatus in the same order. Which three versions are mentioned first? (67*)

h. Sometimes a superscript symbol immediately follows the sign for a manuscript, such as an asterisk in B*. Name at least three of these symbols and describe their functions. (58*–59*)

i. Explain when the abbreviations 𝔐, pm, and Byz are applied. (59*–60*).

j. What does the notation "p)" indicate? (61*)

k. The editors distinguish three groups of Greek manuscripts on the basis of their frequency of citation in the apparatus. What are the technical terms used for these three groups? (61*)

l. Two groups of minuscule manuscripts are combined in "families." What is the sign used to designate these two families? (62*)

m. Two editions of the Majority Text can be identified in the text of Revelation. Which two abbreviations are utilized for these editions? (66*-67*)

n. The editors put an emphasis on noting variants of three old translations. Which ones? (67*)

o. For the Latin version, which two groups of witnesses are to be distinguished? (68*)

p. The Old Latin witnesses are noted in the older editions of the Nestle-Aland in lowercase letters (e.g., a, aur, gig). However, a competing system is used in exegetical literature that ascribes a number to each manuscript. Where can you find a table listing both systems? (69*)

q. References to citations from early Christian writings are listed very selectively in NA28. When are they noted? (78*)

Notes in the Outer and Inner Margins (82*–86*)

a. Three categories of references are added in the outer margin (i.e., the right margin on pages with uneven numbers, the left margin on pages with even numbers). What are they? (82*)

b.   Based on the Two Source Theory, the parallels between Matthew and Luke are distinguished as originating either from Mark or from Q. How did the editors indicate these different dependencies? (82*)

c.   What does the abbreviation "(A)" indicate? (83*)

d.   How are the following writings abbreviated: Matthew, Romans, 1 Corinthians, Hebrews, Acts, and Revelation? (84*)

e.   In the inner margin (i.e., the left margin on pages with uneven numbers, the right margin on pages with even numbers), numbers in italics are sometimes listed (e.g., John 2:1; Rom 1:18). What do these numbers indicate? (85*)

f.   The Eusebian section and canon numbers apply to which writings of the New Testament? (85*)

g.   What is the format of the Eusebian section and canon numbers listed in the inner margin? (85*)

h.   What does an asterisk (*) indicate when it is used in the text line, such as in Luke 3:16? (85*)

The Appendices (86*–88*)

a.   What does an asterisk (*) preceding the abbreviation of a Greek manuscript in the appendix signify, such as in *$\mathfrak{P}^{24}$? (86*)

b.   What do the lowercase letters e a p r stand for? (86*)

c.   Why are the abbreviations "act" and "cath" used intermittently? (86*)

d.   What kind of variant is listed in Appendix II? (87*)

e.   Appendix III lists quotations from and allusions to the Old Testament, the Apocrypha, and non-Christian Greek writers. Why are some references printed in *italics*? (87*)

f.   Where in NA28 are the Latin abbreviations explained? (88*)

2.2. What Is the "Majority Text" (𝔐)?

The term "Majority Text" (𝔐) makes a statement about the frequency of a text variant. It is a fact that at any given place in the text, when all variants are listed, the overwhelming majority of the manuscripts will have the same variant. How can this phenomenon be explained?

The following example may shed some light on this observation. Any copy of the New Revised Standard Version of the New Testament (NRSV) will contain the same English translation word for word. The NRSV has been sold over many years in many different formats, for example, in hardcover, in softcover, as part of study Bibles, and in various electronic formats. Nonetheless, the text in each of these editions is identical. For that reason, a critical apparatus of English translations may reference the text of the NRSV by a single abbreviation.

When it comes to manuscripts, the situation is not so different. Although hand-written copies are much more likely than printed copies to generate textual variations during the transmission process, it is sufficient to reference only the original copy if researchers know that the scribe only tried to reproduce an exemplar and the exemplar he or she tried to copy still exists.

The main reason why so many manuscripts display the same text is that the majority of the surviving manuscripts originate from a relatively late time and from a limited geographic region. Most of the New Testament manuscripts were created in the late Middle Ages, when Greek was no longer used for international communication and when the Byzantine church was able to revise and control the editions of the Greek Bible used in their congregations. Similar to the King James Version for English-speaking audiences, editions were produced that were centrally revised and authorized. Therefore, manuscripts representing a specific Byzantine edition can be referenced by a single abbreviation.

On the other hand, these Byzantine editions clearly preserve old traditions. It would be a severe misunderstanding to presume that the Byzantine editors had invented readings. Although the editing process took place in the Middle Ages, the variants that the editors encountered and documented may have originated in antiquity. Therefore, the readings known to us only through Byzantine manuscripts must not be ignored.

In an attempt to honor recent research on the history of Greek Bible editions, the editors of the *Editio Critica Maior* distanced themselves from the designation "Majority Text" (𝔐). Instead, they applied the term Byzantine text (Byz), which is more precise. This also eliminates the possible misunderstanding of the term "majority" as a quality assessment. Obviously, the fact that a specific text variant is documented more often than other variants does not necessarily indicate that this reading represents the initial text. The number of copies establishes no criterion for the quality of a variant.

2.3. THE TEXT OF THE CATHOLIC LETTERS

From the outset (foreword, vii) the editors make readers of NA28 aware that they approached the text and the apparatus of the Catholic Letters differently than the other writings. The study of text variants and text traditions had advanced further for the Catholic Letters than for the other writings because of the work done on the *Editio Critica Maior* (ECM). To make these new results also accessible to readers of NA28, a degree of inconsistency could not be avoided. Future editions of the Nestle-Aland will reflect the same editorial innovations for the other New Testament writings as soon as that information becomes available.

The editors also introduced a new critical sign, a rhomb (✦), to indicate textual variants for which the decision, whether a reading should go in the text or in the apparatus, could not be reached with the desired certainty. For example, James 1:22 leaves open whether the initial text offered μονον ακροαται or ακροαται μονον. The critical reference in the text is: ✦ ⌐μονον ακροαται⌐. Square brackets [...], used for similar cases in other New Testament writings, are not used within the Catholic Letters.

As mentioned before, the abbreviation for the "Majority Text" (𝔐) is no longer used in the Catholic Letters. Instead, the new and historically more accurate sign "Byz" is introduced to designate the text of standardized Byzantine editions. The distinction of which manuscripts belong to "Byz" varies from writing to writing; they are not listed in NA28. For this information, the ECM must be consulted (see §2.2.2, "Determining the Constant Witnesses for the Catholic Letters," 8*).

Exercise

3   17 Ὑμεῖς δέ, ἀγαπητοί, ⌜μνήσθητε τῶν • ⌜ῥημάτων τῶν   2P3,2
προειρημένων⌝ ὑπὸ τῶν ἀποστόλων τοῦ κυρίου ἡμῶν Ἰη-
σοῦ Χριστοῦ 18 ὅτι ἔλεγον ὑμῖν • ᵀ ⌜ἐπ' ἐσχάτου χρόνου⌝   2P3,3 2T3,1!
⌜ἔσονται ἐμπαῖκται κατὰ τὰς ἑαυτῶν ἐπιθυμίας πορευ-   Is3,4 ⑥·16
όμενοι τῶν ἀσεβειῶν. 19 Οὗτοί εἰσιν οἱ ἀποδιορίζοντεςᵀ,
ψυχικοί, πνεῦμα μὴ ἔχοντες.   Jc3,15!
    20 Ὑμεῖς δέ, ἀγαπητοί, ⌜ἐποικοδομοῦντες ἑαυτοὺς τῇ   Kol2,7!
ἁγιωτάτῃ ὑμῶν πίστει⌝, ἐν πνεύματι ἁγίῳ προσευχόμε-   E6,18
νοιᵀ, 21 ἑαυτοὺς ἐν ἀγάπῃ θεοῦ ⌜τηρήσατε προσδεχόμε-
νοι τὸ ἔλεος τοῦ κυρίου ⌜ἡμῶν Ἰησοῦ Χριστοῦ εἰς ζωὴν⌝   2T1,18
αἰώνιον. 22 °καὶ οὓς μὲν ⌜ἐλεᾶτε διακρινομένους⌝,
23 ⌜οὓς δὲ σῴζετε ἐκ πυρὸς ἁρπάζοντες, οὓς δὲ ἐλεᾶτε   Am4,11 Zch3,2

16 ᵃ𝔓⁷²* | ⌜αυτων ℵ A B* Ψ 5. 33. 81. 88. 307. 1611. 1735. 2344   • 17 ⌜μνημονευετε
1739 | •⌜ προειρημενων ρηματων A 1448. 1611. 1739 sy; Lcf | 18 ᵀ⌜ οτι 𝔓⁷² A C P 5.
33. 81. 88. 307. 436. 442. 642. 1175. 1243. 1448. 1611. 1735. 1739. 1852. 2492 Byz vg sy ¦
txt ℵ B Ψ 2344; Lcf | ⌜επ εσχατου του χρονου ℵ A 33. 436. 1611. 1852 syᵖʰ ᵐˢ·ʰ? ¦ επ
εσχατων των χρονων 442. 2344 boᵐˢˢ ¦ εν εσχατω (+ τω P) χρονω P 88. 642. 1175.
1448ᵛⁱᵈ. 2492 Byz ¦ επ εσχατου των χρονων 81. 307. 1739 (vgˢ) syᵖʰ ᵐˢˢ co ¦ επ εσχατων
του χρονου 1735 ¦ txt 𝔓⁷² B C Ψ 5. 1243 syᵖʰ ᵐˢ·ʰ? | ⌜ελευσονται ℵ² A C 5. 33. 81. 307.
436. 1735. 1739. 2344 vg co ¦ αναστησονται Ψ ¦ txt 𝔓⁷² ℵ* B C* P 88. 442. 642. 1175.
1243. 1448ᵛⁱᵈ. 1611. 1852. 2492 Byz   • 19 ᵀεαυτους C 5. 88. 642. 1243. 1611. 1739ᶜ

NA28, Jude (733).

a. In Jude 18 the editors use a rhomb (•). What variant does
    the critical sign reference, and which text witnesses are
    listed (→ solution)?

b. The rhomb is used only for the Catholic Letters. How
    would the editors reference this variant if it occurred out-
    side of the Catholic Letters (→ solution)?

2.4. Positive and Negative Apparatus

In Jude 18 the text witnesses for the variants in the apparatus are listed
as well as the witnesses supporting the text line; they are separated
by "¦ txt." Entries such as this are called a "positive" apparatus (55*).
In other cases, however, only those witnesses are noted that offer the

variant in the apparatus, and it is up to the reader to determine which manuscripts support the variant in the text line. These entries are referred to as a "negative" apparatus (56*). In case of a negative apparatus, three steps are required to determine the witnesses supporting the reconstructed initial text.

1. Determine the "consistently cited witnesses" as listed in the introduction for the respective writing (61*–67*).
2. Determine whether all consistently cited witnesses contain the text passage, and eliminate those that do not. This information can be found in Appendix I, column 4 (cont.).
3. Finally, eliminate those witnesses that provide the variant indicated in the apparatus.

This method will leave you with a list of manuscripts supporting the variant in the text line. There is one caveat, however. Should the particular page of the manuscript happen to have some minor damage, readers will not be made aware of this, since only major lacunae are noted in Appendix I (56*).

Exercise

a. In Jude 17 the apparatus notes a variant to ῥημάτων τῶν προειρημένων. Which Greek manuscripts support this variant (→ solution)?
b. The critical sign ⊤ at the end of the Lord's Prayer in Matthew 6:13 indicates that some manuscripts have additional text. The King James Version offers the following doxology: "For thine is the kingdom, and the power, and the glory, for ever. Amen." Which manuscripts support this reading (→ solution)?
c. Consider the decision of the editors to treat the doxology of Matthew 6:13 as a later addition. Which general text-critical rule would support this decision (→ solution)?
d. The apparatus for Luke 4:43 indicates a variant in word order. Instead of με δεῖ, the following witnesses have δεῖ με: B (D) W 892. What do the parentheses of the notation

(D) indicate? What is the exact reading of D? How would you proceed to find an answer (→ solution)?

e.   The following witnesses convey the title of the Gospel of John as ευαγγελιον κατα Ιωαννην: C Δ 1424 K Wˢ Θ (A) 565 vgᵂᵂ Ψ ƒ¹ 33 L 700 D 892 𝔓⁷⁵1241 𝔓⁶⁶ 𝔐. Arrange these witnesses in the order as listed in NA28. When you are done, compare your solution with the edition (292) (→ solution).

2.5. THE EARLY TRANSLATIONS

Several early translations of the Greek New Testament survive from antiquity. They are important because translators may have had access to a Greek text of the same quality as our best manuscripts.

However, the editors of NA28 were very cautious and only noted readings for which a strong case could be made that they reflect the readings of a Greek text and that they were not created during the translation process (67*–68*). Special emphasis was put on three languages: Latin, Syriac, and Coptic. Readings from translations into Armenian, Georgian, Gothic, Ethiopic, and Old Church Slavonic were usually not taken into account.

It is important for users of NA28 to understand that the apparatus does not claim to reference exhaustively variants found in early versions. Generally, readings from early translations are listed only when they support variants found in Greek manuscripts. Therefore, it remains impossible to reconstruct the text form of a translation by utilizing the information found in NA28. Providing such information is beyond the scope of a concise edition.

On the other hand, if a variant from a version is noted, users should realize that the editors believe that this variant documents a reading from an old Greek manuscript and that it consequently has the same value for the reconstruction of the initial text as any other Greek manuscript.

2.6. EARLY QUOTATIONS FROM THE NEW TESTAMENT

Quotes from the New Testament found in ancient literature can provide valuable insights into the text of early manuscripts. Working with these references, however, is challenging because it is often difficult to distinguish between allusions and direct quotations and because later scribes copying the writings of early Christian authors often replaced unfamiliar quotes with quotes they found in their contemporary Bibles. The editors of NA28 decided to be cautious and note such citations "only when they can be considered reliable witnesses to the text of the manuscripts quoted" (78*).

The expression "church fathers," traditionally employed for such witnesses, is not always adequate. Some anonymous or forged writings (e.g., Ambrosiaster, a commentary on Paul forged under the name of Ambrosius during his lifetime) may have been written by a woman (a church mother?) and some of the most valuable sources did not originate with supporters of the catholic church but with its critics (e.g., Marcion, Pelagius, Ptolemy). The dates given in the list of "Abbreviations for the Church Fathers" (80*) serve only for a first orientation. The reference of the year is associated sometimes with the time of the author and sometimes with the date of publication of a specific writing. Caution needs to be exercised here as well. For instance, "Ir^{arm}" (the Armenian edition of Irenaeus's writings) is dated to the fourth and fifth centuries, but Irenaeus himself ("Ir") to the second century (80*). Although the Armenian translation was made centuries after the author's death, it is certainly based on Irenaeus's writings, and it may preserve a second-century variant of a New Testament text.

2.7. The Canon Tables of Eusebius

The four Gospels of the New Testament display numerous parallels. The Canon Tables, which Eusebius of Caesarea developed in the fourth century, are a tool for quick identification of such parallel traditions. The so-called *canones* are noted in many Gospel manuscripts and also in NA28. Their value for working with the Greek New Testament is often underestimated.

Eusebius explains his system in his letter to Carpianus, which is reproduced in Greek in NA28 (89*–90*). The most important passages are the following (lines 1–2 and 13–30):

Eusebius to Carpianus, his beloved brother in the Lord. Greetings.

I have put together ten tables for you. The first table contains numbers that reference the parallels in all four Gospels, Matthew, Mark, Luke, and John. The second table correlates the parallels in Matthew, Mark, and Luke, ... the fifth correlates the parallels in Matthew and Luke, [and] ... the tenth marks textual passages that are only in one Gospel.

This is the structure of the tables. They are best used the following way: within the text of the four Gospels numbers have been added that count the sections of each Gospel from beginning to end; at the beginning of each book they start with the numbers one, two, three, until they reach the end of the book. Next to each number an additional numeral is noted in red ink that refers to one of the ten tables.

Instead of applying different colors, the editors of NA28 print the two numerals on top of each other. The upper Arabic number identifies the passage, the lower Roman numeral identifies the table, the so-called canon.

For instance, in the margin of Mark 13:1 the numbers $\frac{137}{II}$ indicate that the text of Mark has reached section number 137, and since the next section 138 begins with Mark 13:3, the number references Mark 13:1–2. The Roman numeral II underneath refers to canon II.

The canon table II is printed on page 91*, "CANON II, IN QUO TRES," and it lists parallels in the three Synoptic Gospels, Matthew, Mark, and Luke.

Exercise

a. Using the Eusebian canon tables, which parallel for Mark 13:1–2 is referenced in Matthew (→ solution)?
b. Using the Eusebian canon tables, which parallels in the Gospel of Luke are referenced for the same section (→ solution)?

Three canons are especially helpful. In the context of the Two Source Theory, the parallels in the first three Gospels are listed in canon II. The parallels between Matthew and Luke, which are not documented in Mark and therefore typically assigned to the Source Q, are listed in canon V.

In the context of redaction-critical approaches, however, passages found in only one Gospel are of particular interest. These sections are listed in canon X.

When it comes to interpreting John, finally, those sections hold a special fascination that are known from the first three Gospels and that are often renarrated with a surprising twist. Such sections are listed in canon I. Canon III lists the parallels between John and Q.

Exercise

c. In the context of the Two Source Theory, Matthew 8 seems to combine passages from Mark with passages from Q. Using the Eusebian canons, which material is possibly from Mark, which possibly from Q, and which passages original to Matthew (→ solution)?

2.8. APPENDIX I B: CODICES LATINI

The same format used for the description of Greek manuscripts in Appendix I (see p. 16) is applied to the Latin manuscripts referenced in the apparatus. They are listed in a table with four columns. Column 1 gives the short designation of the manuscript (ms. nr.), column 2 the century (saec. = *saeculum*), column 3 the holding institution and call number (bibliotheca), and column 4 the content (cont. = *continent*). Different from the list of Greek manuscripts, however, the Latin manuscripts are organized into sections according to their content: Gospels (*evangelia*), Acts (*actus apostolorum*), Letters of Paul (*corpus Paulinum*), Catholic Letters (*epistulae catholicae*), and Revelation (*apokalypsis*). As a consequence, a Latin manuscript that contains more than one collection unit will also be listed in more than one section.

The manuscripts are named by using lowercase letters and a number. Similar to the Greek manuscripts, the same letter may be used for different manuscripts; only the numbers are exact identifiers. For instance, the letter "e" in the Gospels designates manuscript 2 of the fifth century; in Acts, however, "e" refers to manuscript 50 of the sixth century.

Exercise

a. Which Latin manuscript uses the abbreviation "d" (→ solution)?

2.9. Appendix II: Variae Lectiones Minores

To avoid creating an overly long apparatus, variants may not be fully documented in the apparatus when they are related to but not identical with the variant at which they are listed. Instead, these witnesses are noted in parentheses and their readings are given in Appendix II.

Exercise

a. In the apparatus for Romans 15:23 the critical sign ⌐ refers to a variant in F that is not fully explained. Where can you find the exact reading in NA28 (→ solution)?

NA28 AS AN EDITION FOR SCHOLARS

The following comments address strengths and limitations of NA28 as a resource for scholars. They are written for colleagues engaged as academic teachers and researchers who are familiar with previous editions of the Nestle-Aland.

3.1. CHANGES BETWEEN THE 27TH AND 28TH EDITIONS

Editio Minor

Perhaps the greatest difference between the 27th and the 28th editions lies in the Nestle-Aland's new concept of becoming the *editio minor* to the *Editio Critica Maior* (ECM). This concept that has already been realized for the Catholic Letters in NA28, but "[t]he text of the remaining New Testament writings will remain unchanged until progress with the ECM provides the material and knowledge needed for a sustainable revision" (vii). This new concept accounts for the new editorial features reflected in the text and the apparatus of the Catholic Letters that were earlier discussed in detail (see p. 33).

Another consequence of this decision is the expectation that scholars will familiarize themselves with the ECM, since important documentation is only referenced but not repeated in NA28. Particularly questions about methodology and the evaluation of individual witnesses are deferred to the ECM (see the discussion of the Byzantine text, 53*).

Witnesses of the Second Order

The distinction between witnesses of the first and second order has been abandoned (56*). The positive apparatus now lists all consistently cited witnesses. The complicated and occasionally unreliable process of reconstructing the text of witnesses of the second order in previous editions has now become obsolete. Although this change has made the description of the text evidence more exact, it also resulted in longer entries in the apparatus. Furthermore, even consistently cited witnesses, when referenced as part of a "negative apparatus" entry, may still contain an undocumented, small lacuna (see the example below at p. 51, Rom 16:3 in $\mathfrak{P}^{46}$).

Although the editors differentiate three groups of manuscripts (61*), the distinction between consistently cited witnesses, frequently cited manuscripts, and occasionally cited manuscripts is not applied to all parts of the New Testament with the same rigor. The registry of Greek witnesses (61*–67*) lists frequently cited manuscripts only for Acts and for the Letters of Paul; such a distinction has been abandoned for the Gospels, the Catholic Letters, and Revelation, and all listed manuscripts are consistently cited witnesses. Furthermore, the occasionally cited manuscripts are no longer listed for individual writings (62*–67*). Theoretically, however, one could construct such a list by taking all the Greek manuscripts of Appendix I and then subtracting the consistently and frequently cited manuscripts for a specific writing.

The Old Translations

For the old translations, the list of editions on which the collations are based has been updated. Specifically, the editions for the Latin translations of Revelation have changed. Newer Syriac editions have been used to document the text of Syrus Curetonianus (Gospels), the Peshitta (James, 1 Peter, and 1 John), and the Harklensis (Gospels, Letters of Paul, and the Longer Catholic Letters). The references for 2 Peter, 2 John, 3 John, and Jude are based on unpublished collations of the Institute for New Testament Textual Research in Münster. The text of Revelation is quoted using the photographic edition of A. Vööbus (72*).

The nomenclature has changed for the Coptic translations: Subakhmimic (previously ac²) is now Lycopolitanic (ly), and Middle Egyptian Fayyumic (fa) is now Dialect W (crypto-Mesokemic, cw). Fayumic (fa) and Dialect V (cv) are newly introduced designations.

John and Acts are based on collations done at the Institute in Münster when preparing the respective volumes of the ECM for publication.

For the other translations, researchers should take note of the new editions for Ethiopic (Matthew, Acts, Catholic Letters) and for Old Church Slavonic (Gospels) that were consulted.

Dealing with Conjectures

The editors of the NA28 decided to refrain from noting conjectures in the apparatus (49*). The references of previous editions were problematic because they were often kept so brief that it was difficult to identify the source. This was regarded as unsatisfactory, particularly because the selection appeared hardly representative and reflected only older literature. Instead, the notation of conjectures was omitted altogether, and the task of putting together a new register has been now handed over to a group of researchers at the University of Amsterdam (49*).

However, this does not imply that the editors are principally against conjectures. Producing an eclectic text always opens the possibility that in some cases no manuscript containing the original reading has survived. No matter how many text witnesses exist, the initial text may have been lost. Noting theoretical reconstructions of the oldest text form is good practice for editors of eclectic editions.

Inscriptions and Subscriptions

The wealth of variants in the *inscriptiones* and *subscriptiones* of the individual writings of the New Testament is disproportionate to the exegetical yield, so the editors decided no longer to document them (49*).

This commendable editorial decision, nevertheless, has led to the loss of a valuable aspect of previous editions. The subscriptions in the Nestle-Aland allowed for a glance into the history of the New Testament as a publication. For example, the information about where, when, and why each letter of Paul was written was preserved through the mediation of the Byzantine manuscripts in the oldest printed editions and from these in the influential early translations. These notes were part not only of the Luther Bible of 1545 but also of the King

James Version, and they have influenced the understanding of many exegetes and Bible readers well into the twentieth century. A century ago, however, the Bible Societies abandoned the *textus receptus* as the source text for their translations and started to use the Nestle edition, which informed them that the inscriptions and subscriptions were not part of the text but belonged in the apparatus. The inscriptions and subscriptions gradually disappeared from the translations, and now they have been dropped even from most editions of the Luther Bible and the King James Version. NA28 omits them also in the Greek text, even though they are presented in Codex Vaticanus, Codex Sinaiticus, and many other witnesses considered to be of the highest value for reconstructing the initial text.

Abbreviations in the Apparatus

To avoid ambiguities, the apparatus abandons the vague designations *pauci* (*pc*) and *alii* (*al*). Newly introduced is the abbreviation *cf* (*confer*), which replaces the ambiguous *et* ("and") or *sed* ("but").

Textual Changes

One of the most anticipated questions was whether the editors would introduce changes into the text of the Greek New Testament. When the 27th edition appeared, the editors adopted the text of the 26th edition (1979) without changes. Now, for the first time in over thirty years, new variants were introduced in the text line. Since the findings of the Editio Critica Maior (ECM) of the Catholic Letters had been published, the editorial committee decided to adopt the textual decisions of the ECM in NA28 as well (48*).

The thirty-three textual changes within the Catholic Letters are listed separately in the introduction (50*–51*). For nine cases, the previous edition presented variants in square brackets because the editorial committee remained undecided about what to put into the text line and what into the apparatus. Each of these cases has now been decided, and the variant was moved to the apparatus.

The text of the rest of the writings outside of the Catholic Letters remains unchanged and is identical with the text of the 26th and 27th editions.

Appendix I: Greek Manuscripts

NA28 has updated the list of papyri, now recording 127. Compared to the 27th edition, which recorded 116 papyri in its 8th revised reprint of 2001, this growth is impressive.

The 27th edition provided a list of 899 minuscule manuscripts that served as witnesses for the Majority Text; the 28th edition no longer provides such a list.

Appendix II: Variae Lectiones Minores

Under the heading "Variae Lectiones Minores," the 27th edition of Nestle-Aland already provided a list of subvariants that were not fully noted, in order to keep the apparatus shorter. This list has been thoroughly revised.

For instance, the Letter to the Galatians noted fifteen entries in the 27th edition, while the 28th edition reduces the number to eight. Twenty entries for the Letter to the Ephesians are reduced to ten in the 28th edition.

A specific example illustrates the thorough revision this list has undergone: in Galatians 4:11, the first hand of $\mathfrak{P}^{46}$ corrected εκοπισα by inserting an α above the word, εκοπι^{α}σα (for this passage, see Kenyon, 137). This was noted in the 27th edition but omitted in NA28, which no longer traces such subtleties. One of the reasons for eliminating such information is probably the desire to relieve the apparatus from documenting errors that had already been corrected by the first hand at the time of the manuscript's production. For ευαγγελιζηται in Galatians 1:8, variants in 104, 1241^c, 1739*, 0278, and D* had been listed in the 27th edition. In the 28th edition only the reading of D*·c is documented. The variant in 104 was corrected, and it may have been an error in the 27th edition; the correction in 1241 is no longer noted (ημιν is interpreted as an itacism of υμιν); the reading of 1739* is noted as the reading 1739 in NA28 (it may be a correction of the first hand in the manuscript; the entry 1739^{vid} has been omitted); the rearrangement in 0278 is no longer documented in the appendix, only in the apparatus as (^{5} 0278). This brief analysis shows that the information has been carefully checked in the manuscripts with a particular interest in eliminating erroneous readings.

Former Appendix III of the NA27, Editionum Differentiae

The 27th edition included a list that documented the places where the print editions of Tischendorf, Westcott-Hort, von Soden, Vogels, Merk, Bover, and NA25 differ from each other. This list has been omitted in NA28.

Appendix III: Loci Citati vel Allegati

The citations and allusions to passages in the Jewish scriptures and in secular Greek literature that are referenced in the outer margin are systematically listed in Appendix III of NA28. The list has been thoroughly revised and expanded. The thirty-six pages in the 27th edition have grown to forty-two pages. Therefore, scholars accustomed to citing these parallels in their academic instruction should be aware that they have changed considerably and that students using the 27th edition will often find entries that differ from NA28.

Appendix IV: Signa et Abbreviationes

When Eberhard Nestle published his first edition of the *Novum Testamentum Graece* in 1898, he added only four pages of explanations, and they were written in Latin. Although the documentation grew from edition to edition, eventually also with a German and English presentation, it was not until the 26th edition that the editors decided to drop the Latin version. While the system of abbreviations in NA28 remains in Latin, their German and English translations are provided for the first time in Appendix IV.

3.2. LIMITATIONS OF THE NA28

The Nestle-Aland edition of the Greek New Testament is widely used and provides the source text for most contemporary Bible translations; for many scholars and academic teachers the Nestle-Aland text is the only text to use. The impressive success and market acceptance, however, has led some to believe that NA28 documents all known variants and lists all existing manuscripts. Time and again, the editors remind readers that NA28 is a concise edition with the clearly defined goal to provide a "hand edition" (German: *Handausgabe*) for use in academic instruction, scholarship, and church life. As the *editio minor*, it is specifically qualified to supplement the *editio critica maior* (see foreword, vii), which is still many years away from completion and which intends to provide the complete documentation of manuscripts and variants.

The previous sections of this book have described the strengths of the edition and how to use it. The following will discuss the limitations NA28 when used in the context of scholarship. Concrete examples shall highlight some of these issues.

Example: Romans 15:31 in $\mathfrak{P}^{46}$

The text in Romans 15:31 and the corresponding apparatus is reproduced in NA28 as follows (514):

θεόν, **31** ἵνα ῥυσθῶ ἀπὸ τῶν ἀπειθούντων ἐν τῇ Ἰουδαίᾳ καὶ ᵀ ἡ ⸀διακονία μου ἡ ⸆εἰς Ἰερουσαλὴμ εὐπρόσδεκτος τοῖς ἁγίοις γένηται, **32** ἵνα ⸀ἐν χαρᾷ ἐλθὼν⸃ πρὸς

• 31 ᵀ ινα ℵ² D² L Ψ 33. 104. 365. 1175. 1241. 1505 𝔐 f g syʰ; Ambst ¦ *txt* 𝔓⁴⁶ ℵ* A B C D* F G P 6. 81. 630. 1506. 1739. 1881 lat | ⸀δωροφορια B D* F G it; Ambst ¦ *txt* 𝔓⁴⁶ ℵ A C D² L P Ψ 33. 81. 104. 365. 630. 1175. 1241. 1505. 1506. 1739. 1881 𝔐 f g vgᵐˢˢ sy co | ⸆εν B D* F G 1505 ¦ *txt* 𝔓⁴⁶ ℵ A C D¹ L P Ψ 33. 81. 104. 365. 630. 1175. 1241. 1506. 1739. 1881 𝔐 • 32 ⸀εν χαρα ελθω 𝔓⁴⁶ ℵ² B D F G L P Ψ 104. 1175. 1241 𝔐 ¦ ελθων εν χαρα ℵ* ¦ *txt* A C 6. 33. 81. 365. 630. 1505. 1506. 1739. 1881

The editors rank $\mathfrak{P}^{46}$ among the consistently cited witnesses for the text of Romans (63*), and the appendix does not reference a gap for this passage in $\mathfrak{P}^{46}$ (794–95). Of the four places where the editors reference variants, $\mathfrak{P}^{46}$ supports the version reproduced in the text of NA28 three times, and only once does it support the variant noted in the apparatus (ελθω instead of ελθων in 15:32). When reconstructing the wording of $\mathfrak{P}^{46}$ from the information provided by NA28, one would end up with the following wording:

θεον ινα ρυσθω απο των απειθουντων εν τη ιουδαια και η διακονια
μου η εις ιερουσαλημ ευπροσδεκτος τοις αγιοις γενηται ινα εν
χαρα ελθω προς

The passage in 𝔓⁴⁶, however, looks like this (lines 5–8, P.Mich.inv.
6238, 38 verso):

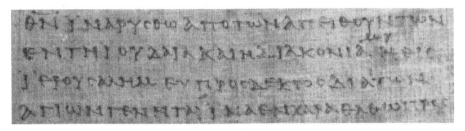

𝔓⁴⁶: P.Mich.inv. 6238,38; Verso (Rom 15:29–16:3). Image reproduced
with the permission of the Papyrology Collection. Graduate Library,
University of Michigan; Inventroy number: P.Mich.Inv. 6238.

The transcription of the passage in 𝔓⁴⁶ is:

θεον ινα ρυσθω απο των απειθουντων
εν τη ιουδαια και η διακονια (*correction:* μου) η εις
ιερουσαλημ ευπροσδεκτος δια των
αγιων γενηται ινα εν χαρα ελθω προς

As was pointed out earlier (p. 6), peculiarities of a specific manuscript
are not documented in NA28. These include the *nomen sacrum* θ̄ν̄ in
the first line and the trema above the first vowel of ϊουδαια, ϊερουσαλημ,
and ϊνα (twice).

A comparison of the transcription of 𝔓⁴⁶ with the text line of
NA28 reveals two differences: instead of δια των αγιων (𝔓⁴⁶), NA28
offers τοις αγιοις in the text of Romans 15:31; instead of ελθω, the
NA28 offers ελθων in verse 32. The second variant is noted for 𝔓⁴⁶ in
the apparatus; the first variant, however, is not.

Interpretation
Users might suspect an error in NA28, thinking that every variant of
every consistently cited manuscript is documented. However, the edi-

tors do not provide a comprehensive list of all known variants to the text of the New Testament. They only intend to document the readings of certain manuscripts at a selection of places.

The example demonstrates three points. (1) For those parts of the text line where the editors did not create an entry in the apparatus, one cannot assume that all consistently cited witnesses support the text. Actually, $\mathfrak{P}^{46}$ is not the only manuscript with a variant to τοις αγιοις γενηται of the NA28 text line. Three other consistently cited witnesses (D, F, G) rearrange the words: γενηται τοις αγιοις (Kenyon, 18). (2) Not all variants of each of the consistently cited manuscripts are recorded in NA28. (3) If the researcher reading a specific manuscript discovers a variant to the text line of NA28 at a place that shows no entry in the apparatus, it is not possible to say whether or not this variant is supported by other manuscripts as well.

Selection of Manuscripts

The decision of selecting certain manuscripts as consistently cited witnesses significantly affects the quality of the reconstructed initial text. A different selection of manuscripts would have resulted in a different critical text. The criteria for the selection of manuscripts as consistently cited witnesses is explained only briefly and in very general terms in the introduction (54*): "the quality and the reliability of the witnesses … are derived from the text-historical place and from the transcriptional character of single witnesses and groups of witnesses." From the 26th edition onward, the assessment of the value of specific manuscripts is based on collations of test passages. In the case of NA28, these collations, together with the critical discussion among a diverse and international board of editors, counteract the danger that the selection of witnesses might reflect the subjective preference of an individual.

With the exception of the general remarks concerning the Catholic Letters (52*–53*), the editors of NA28 do not explain the criteria they applied at each entry to decide which readings were placed in the text line and which were put in the apparatus. Indeed, such clarifications would go beyond the scope of a concise handbook. However, the discussions of editors of older editions are documented in Bruce Metzger, *A Textual Commentary on the Greek New Testament.*

One way of describing NA28 is that it documents the outcome but not the process of the editorial committee of selecting consistently cited manuscripts and of selecting places for making an apparatus entry. Helpful for better understanding the process is Kurt Aland and Barbara Aland, *The Text of the New Testament*. This highly acclaimed work describes a system of categories for New Testament manuscripts based on the collation of test passages that has guided the editorial committee of previous editions in their choice of witnesses and their evaluation of variants.

Selection of Text Passages

The first Nestle editions compared printed editions of the Greek New Testament. Whenever editions agreed, the reading formed the text line; when they disagreed, the minority opinion was noted in the apparatus. The disagreements determined where to make an entry in the apparatus. Over time, however, the evidence from the manuscripts gradually replaced the print editions. Although the places noting variants substantially increased in number from edition to edition, the editors never explained why they would pick a certain place to create an apparatus entry and leave out another place where variants exist. NA28 also provides no rationale for the selection.

Dealing with Lacunae

The difficulties arising from the fact that NA28 does not document minor gaps in manuscripts are best illustrated by a concrete example.

𝔓⁴⁶: P.Mich.inv. 6238,38; Verso (Romans 15:29–16:3). Image reproduced with the permission of the Papyrology Collection. Graduate Library, University of Michigan; Inventory number: P.Mich.Inv. 6238.

As one can see in the photograph of Romans 16:2–4 in 𝔓⁴⁶ on page 50, the lower margin of the page is not completely preserved: text is missing at the right margin of the page, and the bottom line is frayed.

In Kenyon's critical edition of the manuscript (p. 18), the bottom lines of the codex page are transcribed as follows:

χρηζη πραγματι και γαρ αυτη [προστατις
και αλλων πολλων εγεν[ηθη και εμου αυτου
3 ασ]πασασθε πρεισκαν κ[αι ακυλαν τους
4 [συνεργους μου εν χρω ιην οιτινες υπερ]

Letters are missing at the beginning and also at the end of the last visible line. When comparing the text with the text from other manuscripts, it must be furthermore presumed that an entire line of text has been physically lost.

For Romans 16:3 two variants are noted in NA28: Πρισκαν is reproduced in some witnesses as Πρισκιλλαν; and some manuscripts add six words after Χριστω Ιησου; more precisely, six words from Romans 16:5 (και την κατ οικον αυτων εκκλησιαν) are moved to this location. Both apparatus entries are formulated as a so-called "negative apparatus"; that is, the witnesses for the text are not listed, but only the attestation *contra textum* is offered (56*).

χρήζῃ πράγματι· καὶ γὰρ ⌜αὐτὴ ⌐προστάτις πολλῶν ἐγενήθη καὶ ἐμοῦ αὐτοῦ⌐. 3 Ἀσπάσασθε ⌜Πρίσκαν καὶ Ἀκύλαν τοὺς συνεργούς μου ἐν Χριστῷ Ἰησοῦᵀ, 4 οἵτινες ὑπὲρ

• 3 ⌜ Πρισκιλλαν 81. 365. 614. 629. 630. 945. 1505. 1881ᶜ ar m vgᵐˢˢ sy (boᵖᵗ); Ambst | ᵀ και την κατ οικον αυτων εκκλησιαν D*·² F G ar m

Text of and apparatus to Romans 16:3 in NA28 (515).

In such cases one might assume that all consistently cited witnesses, for which no lacunae are noted in the appendix, offer the reading of the text line. Caution is advised. Appendix I notes no gap for $\mathfrak{P}^{46}$ between Romans 15:11 and 16:27 (794). A cursory glance at $\mathfrak{P}^{46}$ indicates, however, that on the six pages containing text of Romans 15:11–16:27 (Kenyon, 16–21: fol. 19–21 verso and recto), the bottom lines are often incomplete and that the lowest line is in fact frequently missing. This is true for the page under consideration.

This leads to the peculiar observation that the conclusion for the first variant ($\mathfrak{P}^{46}$ offering Πρισκαν) is correct; for the second variant, however, $\mathfrak{P}^{46}$ is not a witness, since the entire line is missing.

What does this mean for the readers of the edition? If the wording of a specific manuscript for a specific passage is crucial to an exegetical argument, then the references in the apparatus are not sufficient. This is true particularly for highly fragmented manuscripts. It must not be assumed that all gaps in a manuscript have been referenced. Therefore, caution is advised particularly with a negative apparatus. As soon as an important argument is based on the wording of a certain manuscript, the readings must be examined by using a more exhaustive critical edition, by looking at photographs, or by consulting the original.

Using NA28 to reconstruct the exact wording of a manuscript is not possible. The editors did not intend to provide a tool that documents all readings, differences in orthography, mistakes, illegible words, lacunae, or other peculiarities of each individual manuscript. Only occasionally are such observations noted.

Local-Genealogical Method

The methodology that previously guided the editors in their text decisions has changed in NA28. The term used in previous editions for the methodological approach, the "local-genealogical" method (see Kurt Aland's classic explanation of the "lokal-genealogische Methode" in his introduction to the 26th edition, p. 5*), is no longer used for the 28th edition.

The local-genealogical method constituted an effort to determine at any given place in the text where variants are noted and which of the extant readings is the initial reading. The other variants were then organized in a stemma, like a family tree, depicting how each variant developed from other variants. Usually *stemmata* are constructed to describe the relationship of manuscripts to each other, not to variants. So far, however, all attempts to place New Testament manuscripts in a conclusive stemma have failed. Further, since a stemma of manuscripts is typically based on a small selection of pertinent variants (German: *Leitvarianten*), Kurt Aland and his team suggested that the evaluation of a local-genealogical approach would be an excellent new tool for determining the quality of each manuscript. The manuscripts that have the highest percentage of variants belonging to the initial text, as determined by the local-genealogical method, would in all probability be the best choice of preserving the initial reading in places where a decision could not be made based on a local-genealogical approach. This led to a computer-based analysis and to the development of categories for determining the proximity of a specific manuscript to the initial text. The categories and statistical data were published in Kurt Aland and Barbara Aland, *The Text of the New Testament*.

Coherence-Based Genealogical Method

The local-genealogical approach was further developed into the Coherence-Based Genealogical Method (CBGM), and its first results are now documented for the Catholic Letters. However, the method itself is not explained in detail in NA28 (52*); instead, the editors refer to the essay "Contamination, Coherence, and Coincidence in Textual Transmission: The Coherence-Based Genealogical Method (CBGM) as a Complement and Corrective to Existing Approaches," by Gerd Mink, who developed this method as part of his work at the Institute for New Testament Textual Research in Münster (52* n. 3).

A basic insight of the CBGM is that the initial text is best understood as a virtual text, a text that has not survived in this form in any existing manuscript. Consequently, a stemma of manuscripts must occasionally allow room for postulated manuscripts that have also been lost and that have influenced other manuscripts. These virtual witnesses should be treated with the same validity as existing manuscripts.

Furthermore, the CBGM acknowledges that the text of the surviving manuscripts is contaminated. This means that, during the production and transmission of manuscripts, variants of one manuscript tradition are often blended with variants of another manuscript tradition and that a reconstruction of a conclusive stemma of manuscripts will most likely never be possible.

For the first time in the history of text-critical research, the wealth of variants can be comprehensively described through electronic media. The abundance of data is now waiting for an adequate interpretation. The CBGM resembles a controlled methodical approach to evaluate the established data. Changing philological criteria of recognizing local-genealogical dependencies (so-called genealogical coherence) will also change the results provided by this method.

The CBGM is a "meta-method," a tool promising to help scholars access and evaluate data. It is not designed to produce a stemma of all existing manuscripts; rather, it provides a controlled approach to describe the relationship of individual manuscripts to each other. This method does not make text decisions. It would be a grave misunderstanding to think that the CBGM would let the computer determine the initial text by evaluating all extant variants.

The Institute for New Testament Textual Research offers a portal for interested readers to experiment with this approach (http://intf .uni-muenster.de/cbgm/en.html).

The next decades will show whether the Coherence Based Geological Method will find full acceptance in the discipline. The documentation of data and methodology are important steps for a constructive discussion. Nevertheless, users of NA28 should be aware that a different methodical approach will inevitably produce a different critical text.

APPENDIX: SUGGESTIONS FOR TEACHERS

The following examples demonstrate how NA28 can be used in an academic teaching environment to highlight traditional exegetical problems. The quoted English translations are from the New Revised Standard Version.

WOMEN SHOULD BE SILENT IN THE CHURCHES

An often-quoted section from 1 Corinthians reads:

> Women should be silent in the churches. For they are not permitted to speak, but should be subordinate, as the law also says. If there is anything they desire to know, let them ask their husbands at home. For it is shameful for a woman to speak in church.

The following excerpt reproduces the context. The above section has been removed. Try to identify its original location!

> If a revelation is made to someone else sitting nearby, let the first person be silent. For you can all prophesy one by one, so that all may learn and all be encouraged. And the spirits of prophets are subject to the prophets, for God is a God not of disorder but of peace as in all the churches of the saints. Or did the word of God originate with you? Or are you the only ones it has reached? Anyone who claims to be a prophet, or to have spiritual powers, must acknowledge that what I am writing to you is a command of the Lord. Anyone who does not recognize this is not to be recognized. So, my friends, be eager to prophesy, and do not forbid speaking in tongues; but all things should be done decently and in order.

The passage from 1 Corinthians suggests that members of the congregation who have the gift of prophecy should not all speak at the same time but one after another.

A classroom discussion could focus on the question where to place the excerpt. Some may argue that the passage "Women should be silent in the churches…" disrupts the flow and that the text would read better without it. At some point the group may read the entire passage (1 Cor 14:30–40) in an English translation for additional insights to continue the discussion.

After discussion, the teacher might present a photograph of the passage in Codex Boenerianus (G 012),[2] then ask students to identify and transcribe the passage with the help of NA28. This exercise could serve as homework or as a small-group assignment.

The apparatus of the NA28 informs users that G as well as two other majuscule manuscripts (D, F) present the excerpt ("Women should be silent …") not where current English translations have it (1 Cor 14:33–34) but after 1 Cor 14:40, at the end of the chapter.

Students will probably come up with a range of different explanations for this observation. The ideas that the passage was either inserted later or simply rearranged to improve the flow are discussed in exegetical literature. The former idea is supported by the striking similarities of the passage with 1 Tim 2:11–12, as indicated in parallels noted in the outer margin of NA28. It is therefore possible that the same editors who accepted 1 Timothy into the canonical collection of the Letters of Paul inserted the passage in 1 Cor 14. The latter idea, that an editor of D, F, and G rearranged the passage to make the text flow better, is supported by Romans 16: the apparatus of NA28 indicates that the same group of manuscripts (D, F, G) have rearranged the following passages: in 16:3–5 words are rearranged to improve the flow, and 16:16b is moved to 16:21; and 16:20b is moved to 16:24.

---

2. The University Library of Dresden gives access to the images through their website: http://digital.slub-dresden.de/id274591448; see the top of page [83]-37.

THE ASCENSION STORY IN LUKE

Most contemporary English translations have a note following Luke 24:51: "While he was blessing them, he withdrew from them and was carried up into heaven." The New Revised Standard Version notes: "Other ancient authorities lack *and was carried up into heaven.*"

From an exegetical point of view, the story of the ascension is problematic because the Gospel according to Luke places the event in Bethany on Easter Sunday, whereas the account in Acts has Jesus ascend into heaven from the "Mount called Olivet" forty days after Easter (Acts 1:3, 12). If the ascension narrative of the Gospel of Luke were omitted, the interpretational challenge would be resolved.

Analyzing the apparatus of NA28, students should discover that the Greek words και ανεφερετο εις τον ουρανον originally were not written by the first hand of Codex Sinaiticus (ℵ*). A photograph of the relevant page can be viewed via the website dedicated to this manuscript: codexsinaiticus.org. There the information from the apparatus is easily verified: the words are added in the upper margin of the page.

The student discussion could explore two explanations for the observation: either this omission resulted from an oversight, or it does indeed represent an old, perhaps even the initial, text.

The idea that the variant is a scribal error is supported by the observation that the following text begins with the same four letters that stand at the beginning of the omission: και α. A well-documented copying mistake happens when the eyes of a scribe skip a line because two lines begin with the same sequence of letters.

και ανεφερετο εις τον ουρανον
και αυτοι ...

But the other theory, that this is a very old variant, is supported by the fact that this variant shows up in the oldest Latin and Syriac translations (it sy[s]) as well.

AN ALTERNATIVE EDITION OF ACTS

Just browsing through text and apparatus of Acts in NA28, one may frequently observe longer additions, such as Acts 1:9; 2:1; 3:11–12.

Upon closer examination, it becomes apparent that most of these additions are documented in a single Greek manuscript, Codex Bezae Cantabrigiensis of the fifth century (D 05). Photographs of this manuscript, arguably the most enigmatic witness to the Gospels and Acts, are accessible through a website: cudl.lib.cam.ac.uk/collections/ Christian.

Comparing these variants and identifying similarities can be a rewarding exercise for students. Often these additions try to explain something in the text that requires more background information. For instance, in most manuscript traditions Acts 19:9 reads, "When some stubbornly refused to believe and spoke evil of the Way before the congregation, he left them, taking the disciples with him, and argued daily in the lecture hall of Tyrannus." The apparatus notes a longer reading in D, τινος απο ωρας πεμπτης εως δεκατης ("from the fifth to the tenth hour," i.e., from 11 AM to 4 PM). The variant seems to explain why Paul had access to the lecture hall: during the hottest time of day, no one was using it.

SOLUTIONS TO THE EXERCISES

1.1. Structure and Intention of the Edition

Excursus: For Students without Knowledge of Greek

Reading Exercise (10–11)

a. Ο ασπασμος τη εμη χειρι Παυλου. ει τις ου φιλει τον κυριον, ητω αναθεμα. μαρανα θα. η χαρις του κυριου Ιησου μεθ' υμων. η αγαπη μου μετα παντων υμων εν Χριστω Ιησου.

b. ʿΟ ασπασμος τη εμη χειρι Παυλου. ει τις ου φιλει τον κυριον, ητω αναθεμα. μαρανα θα. ʿη χαρις του κυριου Ιησου μεθ' ʿυμων. ʿη αγαπη μου μετα παντων ʿυμων εν Χριστω Ιησου.

c. ʿΟ ασπασμος τη εμη χειρι Παυλου. ει τις ου φιλει τον κυριον, ητω αναθεμα. μαρανα θα. ʿη χαρις του κυριου Ιησου μεθ' ʿυμων. ʿη αγαπη μου μετα παντων ʿυμων εν Χριστω Ιησου.

Writing Exercise (11)

b. Ο ΑΣΠΑΣΜΟΣ ΤΗ ΕΜΗ ΧΕΙΡΙ ΠΑΥΛΟΥ. ΕΙ ΤΙΣ ΟΥ ΦΙΛΕΙ ΤΟΝ ΚΥΡΙΟΝ, ΗΤΩ ΑΝΑΘΕΜΑ. ΜΑΡΑΝΑ ΘΑ. Η ΧΑΡΙΣ ΤΟΥ ΚΥΡΙΟΥ ΙΗΣΟΥ ΜΕΘ' ΥΜΩΝ. Η ΑΓΑΠΗ ΜΟΥ ΜΕΤΑ ΠΑΝΤΩΝ ΥΜΩΝ ΕΝ ΧΡΙΣΤΩ ΙΗΣΟΥ.

1.3. Looking at One Page of NA28 (13–14))

b. The following parallels for verses 46–52 are noted: Matt 20:29–34; Luke 18:35–43/Matt 9:27–31. (13)

d. The witnesses, which have the four Greek words, Καὶ ἔρχονται εἰς Ἰεριχώ, missing, are noted as: B* saᵐˢ. (13–14)

1.4. STRUCTURE OF THE EDITION

1.4.1. Introduction and Main Body with Text and Apparatus (15, 17)

a.   Jude, a servant of Jesus Christ and a brother of James, To those who have been called, who are loved in God the Father and kept for Jesus Christ: Mercy, peace and love be yours in abundance.

b.   Text (NIV Jude 3): ⌜Dear friends, although I was very eager⌝ to write to you about the salvation we share, I ⌜¹felt compelled⌝ to write and ⌜urge you to contend for the faith that was once for all entrusted to ⌜² God's holy people⌝. Apparatus: ⌜Beloved, while eagerly preparing | ⌜¹ find it necessary | ⌜appeal to | ⌜² the saints.

c.   Papyri: 𝔓⁵⁶ᶜ. Majuscules: ℵ A B C* Ψ. Minuscules: 81. 323. 945. 1175. Translation: lat. Citation: Eus.

1.4.2. Appendices (21)

a.   The last part of Hebrews (from 9:14 to the end), 1 Timothy, 2 Timothy, Titus, and Philemon are missing. Since "r" is not mentioned as one of the four parts of the New Testament (e a p r), the Revelation of John is missing as well.

b.   Information given in the fourth column answers this question. The same uppercase letter may be assigned for two or more different manuscripts, if each of these manuscripts contains different parts of the New Testament. D 05 combines two collection units, the Gospels (e) and the Praxapostolos (a: Acts and Catholic Letters), while D 06 contains the Letters of Paul (p). Readers are expected to consult the appendix to find out whether an uppercase letter designates more than one manuscript.

c.   The information is given on page 802: *Γ 036 / X / Oxford, Bodl. Libr., Auct. T. inf. 2.2; St. Petersburg, Ross. Nac. Bibl., Gr. 33 / e (vac. Mt 5,31–6,16; 6,30–7,26; 8,27–9,6; 21,19–22,25; Mc 3,34–6,21).

A possible solution that only uses information available in NA28 could read as follows: Majuscule Γ 036 is a copy of the four Gospels. The following sections are missing: Matt 5:31–6:16; 6:30–7:26; 8:27–9:6; 21:19–22:25; Mark 3:34–6:21. Part of the manuscript is currently located in Oxford (Bodl. Libr., Auct. T. inf. 2.2), and another part is in St. Petersburg (Ross. Nac. Bibl., Gr. 33). The appendix of NA28 dates the manuscript to the tenth century.

1.6. CONCLUDING QUESTIONS (25)

a. (1) Greek manuscripts (papyri, majuscules, minuscules, lectionaries), (2) early translations, (3) quotes.
b. Appendix IV provides a comprehensive list, but the full explanations are given in the introduction to the edition.
c. In the back of NA28 (Appendix I).
d. (1) Codex Sinaiticus (ℵ 01), fourth century, British Library in London. (2) Codex Alexandrinus (A 02), fifth century, British Library in London. (3) Codex Vaticanus (B 03), fourth century, Vatican Apostolic Library in Rome. (4) Codex Ephraemi rescriptus (C 04), fifth century, Bibliothèque Nationale in Paris.

2.1. QUESTIONS ABOUT THE INTRODUCTION OF THE EDITION

Foreword (27)

a. The edition of the Catholic Letters reflects a new editorial concept.
b. The references to parallels in the outer margin have been revised for the entire edition.

About the History of the Edition: The 28th Edition (27–28)

a. Two tasks had to be accomplished: (1) The apparatus was revised to give it more clarity and to make it easier to use. (2) The insights and decisions resulting from the work on the *Editio Critica Maior* should be integrated.

b. Because the work on the Editio Critica Maior had arrived at several different text decisions compared to the 27th edition of the Nestle-Aland, and because the editors wanted NA28 to reflect these changes.

c. The chart (50*-51*) lists thirty-three places where the text was changed.[3]

d. The rhomb (✦) marks passages in which the editors left the decision open which variant represents the initial text.

e. It is: Byz.

The Text of the Edition (28)

a. An eclectic text evaluates extant variants with the help of external and internal criteria.

b. Internal criteria are defined as "intrinsic coherence of the text, its grammatical structure and its stylistic, linguistic and theological features" (54*). External criteria are "derived from the text-historical place and the transcriptional character of single witnesses and groups of witnesses" (54*).

c. The Coherence-Based Genealogical Method (CBGM) (52*).

d. Brackets indicate that the editors left open whether or not the variant was part of the initial text. In the Catholic Letters, such passages are marked with a rhomb (✦).

e. The double-brackets ⟦...⟧ mark text passage that, in the opinion of the editors, did not form part of the initial text.

f. Quotations from the Old Testament are printed in italics.

The Critical Apparatus (28–29)

a. The positive apparatus lists the witnesses for the variants in the text line as well as the witnesses with different read-

---

3. In its first printing (2012), thirty-four textual changes were listed. However, one of those changes (ἀλλ' instead of ἀλλά in 1 Pet 2:25) was just orthographical and reflected an attempt to standardize the spelling in the Nestle-Aland. It was listed by mistake.

ings. The negative apparatus lists witnesses for variants that differ from the text line.

b. Punctuation variants.

c. Text between ⸆ ... ⸌ is presented in a different order in some witnesses. The critical sign indicates that a text was moved to a different location.

d. • before a bold number marks the beginning of the next verse.

e. In Appendix II.

f. Punctuation variants.

g. The first versions are listed in the order: Latin, Syriac, Coptic.

h. See pages 14* and 15* of NA28.

i. 𝕸 is applied only outside the Catholic Letters, and it designates the variant that is preserved in the majority of manuscripts. The abbreviation pm (*permulti* = "very many") is applied instead of 𝕸 if the majority of manuscripts is split into two or three groups of about the same size featuring competing variants. Byz replaces the abbreviation 𝕸 in the Catholic Letters and designates more precisely manuscripts associated with Byzantine editions. Byz^pt is used if the Byzantine tradition is not uniform.

j. The notation "p)" characterizes variants that the editors attribute to a parallel in another canonical Gospel. These variants are not considered to be part of the initial text.

k. The three groups are consistently cited, frequently cited, and occasionally cited manuscripts.

l. The abbreviations are: f^1 and f^{13}.

m. 𝕸^A is used for manuscripts that present the text of Revelation as part of the Commentary of Andreas of Caesarea. 𝕸^K designates pure text manuscripts. The superscripted K is a terminological remnant of earlier Nestle editions in which manuscripts, which later were associated with the Majority Text 𝕸, had been termed as Koine manuscripts and designated with the abbreviation 𝕶.

n. Emphasis is given to Latin, Syriac, and Coptic versions.

o. Manuscripts are distinguished between Old Latin translations emerging from the second century onward and manuscripts containing the Vulgate, which dominated the medieval tradition and which are commonly associated with the translation work of Jerome (fourth and fifth centuries).

p. In Appendix I, section B: Codices Latini (815–20), the first column under *ms.nr.* also notes the standardized numbers next to the lowercase letters (exception: t) assigned to the manuscript.

q. Quotations are only noted when the editors are convinced that the citations reference readings found in Greek New Testament manuscripts of the time.

Notes in the Outer and Inner Margins (29–30)

a. (1) Parallels and doublets within other New Testament writings. (2) Quotations from and allusions to Old Testament texts. (3) Parallels but not necessarily quotes in biblical and Jewish literature.

b. A forward slash (/) organizes the parallels into subgroups.

c. The variant is found in the Old Testament section of Codex Alexandrinus.

d. Gospel of Matthew: Mt; Romans: R; 1 Corinthians: 1K; Hebrews: H; Acts: Act; Revelation: Ap.

e. The cursive numbers refer to a system of structuring the text, so-called *kephalaia*. They are designed for quick identification of specific passages.

f. To the four Gospels.

g. The notations consist of an Arabic numeral with a Roman numeral set underneath. The Arabic numerals designate the sections of a Gospel; the Roman numerals indicate charts that reference the parallel sections in the other Gospels that were first established by Eusebius of Caesarea in the fourth century.

h. The little star is used when the beginning of a new chapter of the *kephalaia* does not coincide with the beginning of a verse.

The Appendices (30)

a. The designation signifies that the manuscript is a consistently cited witness.

b. The lowercase letters designate the four parts of the New Testament that are reflected in the manuscript tradition: e = Gospels, a = Praxapostolos (Acts and Catholic Letters), p = Letters of Paul (including Hebrews), r = Revelation of John.

c. When the Praxapostolos (a) is not contained in its entirety, for example, in fragmentary manuscripts, Acts is noted as "act" and the Catholic Letters as "cath."

d. When the critical apparatus notes a witness in parentheses, its exact wording is given in Appendix II.

e. Quotations are set in italics; allusions are printed in regular type.

f. In Appendix IV.

2.3. The Text of the Catholic Letters (33)

a. The οτι is added in papyrus 72; the majuscules A, C, P; the minuscules 5, 33, 81, 88, 107, 436, 442, 642, 1175, 1243, 1448, 1611, 1735, 1739, 1852, 2492; and Greek Byzantine manuscripts, Vulgate manuscripts, and Syriac manuscripts. The text without οτι is offered by the majuscules ℵ, B, Ψ, the minuscule 2344, and Lucifer. The editors left the decision open whether οτι is part of the initial text or whether it originated during the transmission of the text.

b. Before the rhomb was introduced, the 27th edition notes this variant as: °[οτι].

2.4. Positive and Negative Apparatus (34–35)

a. The variant ῥημάτων τῶν προειρημένων in Jude 17 is witnessed by the following Greek manuscripts: 𝔓72; ℵ (01), B (03), C (04), P (025), Ψ (044); 5, 33, 81, 88, 307, 436, 442, 642, 1175, 1243, 1735, 1852, 2344, 2492.

Process: (1) The first step is to eliminate the consistently cited witnesses for Jude that do not have the verse. (2) Witnesses attesting to the variant in the apparatus are eliminated. The consistently cited witnesses for Jude are (23*): $\mathfrak{P}^{72}$, $\mathfrak{P}^{74}$, $\mathfrak{P}^{78}$; ℵ (01), A (02), B (03), C (04), P (025), Ψ (044); 5, 33, 81, 88, 307, 436, 442, 642, 1175, 1243, 1448, 1611, 1735, 1739, 1852, 2344, 2492. Of these, the following do not have text for Jude 17 (Appendix I): $\mathfrak{P}^{74}$, $\mathfrak{P}^{78}$. The apparatus lists as witnesses to the variant of the text line: A 1448. 1611. 1739.

b. The variant is documented in the majuscules K, L, W, Δ, Θ; the minuscules of the manuscript family f^{13}; a correction in minuscule 288; the minuscules 33, 565, 579, 700, 892, 1241, 1424; the lectionary 844; and the Majority Text ($\mathfrak{M}$).

c. Assuming that the doxology would offer a better ending for the Lord's Prayer, the *lectio difficilior potior* may be applied.

The *lectio brevior potior* could explain the version of the Majority Text as a conflation of the short variant (ℵ, B, and D) with a tradition containing the doxology.

The editors also note that the doxology may allude to 1 Chronicles 29:11–13. The Greek text of this passage uses the terms βασιλευς (not βασιλεια), δυναμις, δοξα and αιων.

d. The text of D, as indicated by information from NA28, is: ο δε ειπεν προς αυτους οτι δει με και ταις ετεραις πολεσιν ευαγγελισασθαι την βασιλειαν του θεου οτι ...

Process: Witnesses noted in parentheses in the apparatus offer a variant related to the one where they are listed (58*). The wording of the variant is listed in the Appendix II: Variae Lectiones Minores. The corresponding entry to Luke 4:43 reads: • 43 ^{5} *pon.* δει με *p.* προς αυτους οτι D (824); that is, the manuscript D puts (pon. = *ponit*) δει με behind (p. = *post*) the words προς αυτους οτι.

e. Solution: $\mathfrak{P}^{66}$ $\mathfrak{P}^{75}$ (A) C D K L W^{s} Δ Θ Ψ f^{1} 33 565 700 892 1241 1424 $\mathfrak{M}$ vg^{ww}.

2.7. The Canon Tables of Eusebius (37–38)

a.   Matthew 24:1–2. Process: (1) The number 137 for Mark appears in the middle queue of the third column of CANON II (91*). To the left, 242 indicates the respective section in Matthew. (2) When browsing through Matthew, the number 242 is found at Matthew 24:1. Since the next section 243 begins with Matthew 24:3, the parallel in the Gospel of Matthew, referenced in Mark 13:1–2, is: Matthew 24:1–2.

b.   Luke 19:44 and Luke 21:5–6. Process: The number 137 for Mark appears twice, one below the other, in the middle queue of the third column of CANON II (91*). To the right, two sections are indicated for the Gospel of Luke: 237 and 248. These numbers are shown in NA28 at the inner margin of Luke 19:44 and Luke 21:5–6.

c.   Originating from Q is the healing of the centurion's servant in Capernaum (Matt 8:5–13) and the words about followers of Jesus (Matt 8:18–22). All other text passages are taken from Mark.

Process: The *canones* subdivide Matthew 8 into seven sections (64–69). Three of them are preserved in all three Synoptic Gospels (Canon II). Therefore, they originate from Mark (64; 67; 69). Four sections are missing in Mark but are part of Matthew and Luke, and according to the Two Source Theory they probably originate from Q (Canon III: 64 and V: 65; 66; 68).

2.8. Appendix I B: Codices Latini (39)

a.   Manuscript d in the Gospels, in Acts, and in the Catholic Letters refers to manuscript 5 of the fifth century. In the Letters of Paul, however, manuscript d references the manuscript 75 of the fifth and sixth centuries.

9. Appendix II: Variae Lectiones Minores (39)

a. The reconstruction of Romans 15:22–23 in F reads: διο και ενεκοπτομην πολλακις του ελθειν προς υμας απο πολλων ετων ως αν ουν νυνι δε μηκετι τοπον εχω εν τοις κλιμασιν τουτοις επιποθιαν δε εχων του ελθειν προς υμας.

Process: Appendix II indicates that, regarding this passage, the words απο πολλων ετων ως αν ουν were moved from 15:23–24 to verse 22 after the words προς υμας. Furthermore, the apparatus indicates that in verse 22 τα πολλα was replaced by πολλακις, and in verse 23 εχω replaces εχων.

WORKS REFERENCED

Aland, Barbara, Kurt Aland, Gerd Mink, Holger Strutwolf, and Klaus Wachtel, eds. *Novum Testamentum Graecum: Editio Critica Maior 4, Die Katholischen Briefe.* 2nd ed. Stuttgart: Deutsche Bibelgesellschaft, 2013.

Aland, Kurt, and Barbara Aland. *The Text of the New Testament: An Introduction to the Critical Editions and to the Theory and Practice of Modern Textual Criticism.* 2nd ed. Translated by Erroll F. Rhodes. Grand Rapids: Eerdmans, 1995.

Kenyon, Frederic G. *The Chester Beatty Biblical Papyri.* Vol. 3: *Pauline Epistles: Text.* London: Emery Walker, 1936.

Metzger, Bruce. *A Textual Commentary on the Greek New Testament.* 2nd ed. Stuttgart: Deutsche Bibelgesellschaft, 1994.

Mink, Gerd, "Contamination, Coherence, and Coincidence in Textual Transmission: The Coherence-Based Genealogical Method (CBGM) as a Complement and Corrective to Existing Approaches." Pages 141–216 in *The Textual History of the Greek New Testament.* Edited by Klaus Wachtel and Michael W. Holmes. SBLTCS 8. Atlanta: Society of Biblical Literature, 2011.

CPSIA information can be obtained at www.ICGtesting.com
Printed in the USA
BVOW08*0537190516

448572BV00003B/135/P